HOW WOMEN DEFIED THE ODDS AND SUCCEEDED IN BUSINESS, MINISTRY, AND LIFE

WALK
IN YOUR PURPOSE!

COMPILED BY:

DR. LILY L. JENKINS

Walk in Your Purpose

How Women Defied the Odds and Succeeded in Business, Ministry, and Life

Compiled by Dr. Lily Jenkins

Published by Asta Publications

P.O. Box 1735 | Stockbridge, GA 30281

1-800-482-4190 | www.astapublications.com

Published in the United States of America
ISBN: 978-1-934947-19-7

Table of Contents

Walking in Purpose

By Marita A. DeMarinis

Today I stand before you
A broken woman with an imperfect past
Filled with many tears and trials
From the storms of this life

Walking in Purpose and Plan
For this is my Destiny this Land

I praise my King for the miracles of today
And the promises of tomorrow
For never leaving me or forsaking me
I am blessed everyday, in every way
Even when the clouds are grey
Ever present with me in my darkest days

A page of my past...
A page of future...

Walking in Purpose and Plan
For this is my Destiny in this Land

Crawling, falling, getting back up
Walking in His divine grace
Never losing pace or turning about face
I must persevere and finish this race

A testimony of His Glory, His Greatness
His Undeniable Love
For always loving me
When I didn't always love Him

I praise my Lord and Savior Jesus Christ
For His Father giving Him as a Living Sacrifice
To die just for me
So I could live and have eternal life

Praise, Honor, Glory unto You!
Armed with a garment of praise
An unshakable faith that can't be erased
His special favor, which is His Grace
For this is the reason
I have been saved
Walking in Purpose and Plan
For this is my Destiny in this Land

Today with tears upon my face
The pain and trials of this life
I now embrace
For when I am weak
I am strong through Christ
As my future has already sufficed
My Book of Life already written
By the Ultimate Living Sacrifice

Walking in Purpose and Plan
For this is my Destiny in this Land

Today I worship my Lord and Savior
The Great I AM
The King of Kings
The Lord of Lords
The Alpha, The Omega
The Maker, The Creator
The Author, The Finisher of my faith
Great Counselor, Awesome Teacher
Divine Healer and Deliverer You are
Every knee will bow
And proclaim Your Name...near and far!

Today I stand before you
Purpose Plan Destiny in hand
Not my will but His will written in the sand
My Walk in Purpose predestined before my birth
To go make disciples upon
This beautiful God given earth

His voice sounds from Heaven
Your past is gone...
Your future is bright...
You are my Victorious masterpiece
Created anew in Christ Jesus tonight

Let me sing to the Heavens
Glorifying Your Holy Name
Today, I worship my Lord and King

Walking in Purpose and Plan
For this is my Destiny in this Land

Tangela Ray
Author of Transition

Tangela Ray is a Certified Etiquette Consultant, Lifestyle Coordinator, and Dynamic Inspirational Speaker who believes, *"You Never Get a Second Chance to Make a Great First Impression"*. She is passionate about service, and helping others become the best versions of themselves. Tangela facilitates workshops designed to nurture and empower the human spirit.

She resides in Memphis, Tennessee. You may reach her on her website: **www.tangelrayspeaks.com,** Twitter: @tangelaray, or by phone: 901-834-4414.

STORY 1

Transition

Transition
Tran*si*tion

1. a: passage from one state, stage, subject, or
   place to another: change.
   b: a movement, development, or evolution
   from one form, stage, or style to another.

A decade ago, I anxiously sat across a long table filled with five women and one gentleman all waiting to fire away questions at me to give each of them insight as to whether or not I was the candidate best suited to work for their organization. The very first question set the tone. "Ms. Ray, looking at your resume, you appear to be over-qualified for the position you are applying for." I beamed inside at the recognition of my previous achievements. However, her follow-up was slightly confusing. "May I ask whose job you are really after?" Needless to say, I was stunned. She continued, "You see, Ms. Ray, around here, there is very little room for growth and I can't imagine you would be satisfied in that position with its pay. People in positions like ours don't leave. So if you are after a position other than the one you've applied for, that won't happen." In my mind, the interview was over so I threw caution to the wind and replied, "With all due respect, in my world, things change. People relocate, have babies, retire, get fired; heck, they even die."

After an uncomfortable moment of silence, the gentleman seated at the table asked me a two-part question. "Ms. Ray, why did you apply for this position, and where do you see yourself in five years?" I gladly replied, "I applied for this job to fine tune my public speaking skills. My five year plan is to be self-employed."

A final question was asked by a really sweet, demure lady sitting directly across from me. "Ms. Ray, what do you think you could bring to this organization?" My reply was, "A breath of fresh air." I left the interview upset and unimpressed by the first question. I thought, How unprofessional and what a waste of my time. A month later, I received a call announcing I had been given the job. I was surprised and elated.

My elation would be quickly deflated, however. The dream job to my five-year plan to become skilled in public speaking would instead become a seven-year nightmare. There were gossiping, backstabbing, and write-ups. Then, I was transferred to different departments often out of spite. Every morning, on the way to work, I'd have an upset stomach not knowing what drama the day would bring. On the way home, my thoughts were filled with fear of what was to come tomorrow. My work environment was hostile. I knew there were laws to protect me, so I went to the top for help. I assumed things were resolved, but it actually backfired on me. Co -workers began distancing themselves for fear of retaliation or losing their jobs. There was a target on my back and unless you wanted one on yours too, the word was 'stay away from Tangela; she's a trouble maker'.

My cry became Lord what next? One evening after leaving and arriving home, my ninety-three year old grandmother asked as she always did. "How was your day?" I told her it was awful and began to cry. After several days of giving the same response to that question, Mother (as I called her) asked me, "What job would you like to have?" I paused and said, "I would like to be a highly sought after, world renowned, professional speaker. Mother then said, "Oh, that's nice. What would you speak about? What's your message?"

That was a great question since, at that time, I had absolutely no idea. I simply knew I had a way with people, and in some way, I wanted to share information and be of service to those around me. Not to mention travel the world while sleeping in luxury hotels.

What came next changed me forever. My grandmother asked, "Have you asked God?" And my answer was a quick yes since I had done that. Visibly pleased with my response, my grandmother then gives me this really mischievous 'cat that stole the canary smile' and said, "That is why you are there … to get your message. You can't become a speaker if you don't have anything to speak about. When you go into that building tomorrow, ask God to reveal the lesson to you?"

That was my 'Aha' moment. I had a covenant with God and I broke it. I asked for a position that would allow me to become a better speaker. He gave it to me. Five years were the deal. Instead of seeing that the real validation had already come from God, I tried to fit in. I tried to get my seat at the table in the girls club that was not accepting applications. I had begun looking for their approval and acceptance. Forgetting it had already been written that I could and would become that highly sought after speaker God said I could become. God was sending me into a burning building to get the lesson.

Now what was the lesson? Day in and day out, I discovered the truth that a position does not erase pain. Yes, I walked into a building of highly skilled and powerful women who were all in transition and in pain. Their careers were on track, but their lives were a mess. These women, who were unable to mentor me or anyone else, because they feared losing their position and significance, were validated by their positions and dreaded anyone new coming in replacing them. My "lesson" was to see the pain in them, understand the pain, teach others to recognize it, and heal from the wounds caused by the pain.

> The Gift
> from God
> was the job.
>
> ∞
>
> I was to go in,
> get the training,
> and LEAVE!

Once the lesson was learned, I was to plan my exit and make my own transition. Sounds simple, right? Not so. I was in such a toxic environment for so long that my thinking became toxic. Fear of my unknown had set in. During my time there, I began to doubt what I knew I could do. What I was born to do. After getting the message, I stayed too long and suffered the consequence. I began to make excuses about why I should stay at the very place which was causing me so much emotional pain. Truth was, I was afraid to step out on my own at 44-years-old and become self-employed. Their fears became my fears. I began to live up to the labels others placed on my life. I got off track. One of my major justifications for staying sounded great. I needed medical and dental benefits. Yes, who doesn't, right? Then it hit me like a ton of bricks! My first and very clear message from God was, "If you think that it has been those medical and dental benefits that have sustained you thus far, then you don't know who I Am!" Wow! In 44 years I had not been ill. No surgeries. Yet, medical and dental became my major excuse. Yes, God...message received. There were several powerful lessons I learned along the way. First…I asked God for a job that would prepare me to fulfill my five-year plan. Wish granted. God does what he says he will. Second…Hurt people really do hurt other people. Third…Don't stay too long. Because I stayed too long, I became one of the wounded by those that were hurting. When I refused to leave, things got progressively worse. People became meaner, and in some ways so did I. I became one of them. We were at a standoff. They had no real reason to fire me since all of my performance reviews where stellar. Amid all the emotional stress of the job, God had enabled me to be faithful in any position I was placed in. Isn't God good?!

Though they were in control and could have set me up to fire me, God controlled the pen. My reviews were almost perfect and I always received an increase in pay. Only God! Yes, I should have left at the five-year mark, but I stayed.

Then came the nudge—better yet the push. Out of nowhere … layoffs. I was the very first to get walking papers. Inside, I searched for the "why?" I was cut to the core. I did not see that coming. I felt betrayed. Why was this allowed to happen? Simple… I stayed too long. God had already blessed and equipped me with what I needed to make my transition and I missed it.

The gift from God was the job. I was to go in, get the training, and leave. Instead, I went in looking to be mentored and nurtured by others. I felt like they won, so I initially refused to go. I was wrong. The non-profit organization had to do layoffs to justify a multi-million renovation. When my former employer chose to lay me off first before anyone else a full year and a half before the process started, I thought it was public humiliation being the first to leave, but again I see in hindsight that it was another gift. My severance package and unemployment was my safety net which allowed me the luxury of getting away from the drama and allowing time for me to hear God speak about my future. This two-fold

Without
GOD'S
Grace and Mercy
I may have become
bitter and fearful
about **each** NEW
Transition.

blessing included my being placed into the job market before the others. Secondly, it gave me the extra push I needed to work on developing myself and speaking endeavor.

From my life's journey, I have discovered what I do best is empowering women to be their absolute best outwardly and inwardly. What better lesson could I have been taught in my personal fiery trial? The grass is not always greener, and you never know the pain hiding behind the smiles.

As I reflect, I remember seeing first-hand women in emotional and mental pain hurting other women. I saw their pain, experienced their pain, but thank God I survived their pain. Now as a speaker, I accept the assignment to open dialogue about the fears of transition and circular pain so we can break the cycle. That was my biggest gift from God. Now at the end of my speaking engagements, I look forward to the young, impressionable women who come to share their stories, shake my hand, and ask to be mentored, or seek insight into the speaking business.

God did not allow me to be permanently scarred. Now I smile, just like Mother, and thank God for his grace and mercy because without it, I may have become bitter and fearful about each new transition I still face as I journey onward. I will graciously pass the baton knowing that my assignment has been fulfilled, and I am ready to receive my next assignment for a job well done. In closing, glean strength and support from the truths God taught me.

- Ask God if he is in agreement with what you want
- Accept your answer
- Keep your covenant
- Look for the lesson
- Don't stay too long
- Enjoy your transition; that is the GIFT

I am so happy you purchased our book. Your life can become a true expression of love, grace, and dignity. It is my prayer that our stories place you all on the path to receiving the validation you deserve, the love you desire, and the success we all crave.

Reketta Wright
Author of Flourishing Past Failures

Reketta Wright is a Licensed Professional Counselor specializing in individual, couples, and family therapy. She is passionate about empowering and inspiring women in discovering their authentic self. She teaches women, moms, and entrepreneurs how to succeed in family, business, and life while living a balanced life. For booking or additional information, please visit **www.rekettawright.com** or email **reketta@ rekettawright.com**.

STORY 2

Flourishing Past Failures

Since I can remember I've always loved helping other people. I recall helping my cousins break up arguments when we were younger, and helping friends solve problems later in life. Growing up, my parents instilled in me that education is the key to a successful future, and to always try my best, no matter what I am faced with. After high school graduation, in 2000, I attended college at Winston-Salem State University in Winston-Salem, North Carolina, where I wanted to become an Occupational Therapist. I was accepted into the program and did well in most of my classes. During one particular final exam portion, I couldn't recall several mental health terms and diagnoses, so I failed the final exam. My department chair allowed me to re-take my exam after having an intense meeting with her.

Therefore, I studied diligently for my re-take exam, knowing that I had to pass this exam to further my education in this program. Well, the day finally arrived where I was to complete the exam. I recall having several emotions such as feeling nervous, anxious, and afraid because this one test depended on so much.

I took the test as relaxed as I could, hoping and praying that I would pass. A few days went by and I didn't know if I had passed. I remember receiving a letter in my campus mailbox stating that I needed to schedule another meeting with the Dean of Health Sciences. I thought to myself, what could this mean? I scheduled the meeting for the same week. I met with her, and we reviewed and discussed my retake exam. I failed the exam. I was so disappointed in myself, and I felt as if it was the end of my world. During my meeting, my dean explained that I would be terminated from the program and I would have to switch my major effective next semester.

I was embarrassed, disappointed, and ashamed of myself for failing a re-take exam and getting kicked out of the Occupational Therapy program. I was not used to failing. I had always been an over-achiever from elementary to high school. I thought about how I would call home to my parents and tell them I was expelled from the Occupational Therapy program. As a result, I would have to extend my time in college by a year, and it would cost more money. I remember calling home and speaking to my parents; I was so nervous. I had to deliver this disappointing news. I can remember crying and saying, "I don't know what else I want to major in. I failed my final exam for Occupational Therapy." My parents, being supportive, comforted me and said, "It's okay, things happen. At least you can continue in school." I felt so relieved to have this type of support.

My parents encouraged me to talk with my advisor so that she can help me find something comparable to the helping field. After our conversation ended, I immediately contacted my advisor and scheduled an advisement meeting to review other programs at my university. Once my advisor and I met, I was able to find another program that my courses transferred to and would have helped me to graduate in May 2005, and that program was

Rehabilitation Studies. I entered into the new program, comprehended the courses well, and learned a significant amount on mental health diagnosis, something which I had previously failed. I began to take tests about diagnosis and passed them. I completed projects and did very well. I always had in the back of mind my failure on the final exam in Occupational Therapy but I passed these with flying colors. I finally forgave and stopped being so hard on myself so that I could really enjoy the new program that I was in. Furthermore, I later graduated in May, 2005 to receive my bachelor of science in Rehabilitation Studies.

I've always been an active learner so I wanted to further pursue my passion in helping people. Therefore, I continued my studies to pursue my Master's degree in counseling. I enrolled at North Carolina A&T State University in order to obtain a Master's degree in Rehabilitation Counseling in the fall of 2005. During this transition from college to graduate school, I began to embark on a journey of self discovery. I met new friends, tried new foods, went new places, and I landed my first professional job in 2005 working as an Associate Professional for a private mental health agency in Winston-Salem, North Carolina.

There, I was able to apply what I learned in my undergraduate studies to work with children who had mental health problems. I was their support and taught my clients coping skills as an Associate Professional. My supervisor at the agency was also my peer in the same graduate school program. A year later in spring 2006 after we had developed a friendship and started to learn about each other's strengths more, my peer approached me about a business partnership opportunity. She desired to open an agency similar to the one we both worked in. I was excited and honored that someone saw something in my character to want me to enter into a partnership with her. I was excited about this opportunity because I would become a leader, an entrepreneur, and catalyst in the lives of others. A few months later, we asked another peer in our program to join us in the partnership. We started the planning and developing of our agency from the information and skills we already had. We were both full-time graduate students, but we both wanted more for our lives and families to come, so we met on weekends, sought consultants, and met after classes to work on the initial business planning.

There was so much to be done with starting a new business. I asked myself: what have I gotten myself into? Attending school full-time, working two part-time jobs, now starting a business. I thought all of this was more than I could handle. We didn't give up. We divided parts into our strengths such as: policy development, networking, and research. My role and title was Chief Executive Officer. We combined our start up money from our graduate refund checks. Our first office was located at one of my partner's home in a bedroom. We started with a locked file cabinet, computer, and desk. It took five months for us to get approved from the state. There was a long waiting process, especially for novice entrepreneurs.

While waiting, we determined how we would get clients, bill for services, and hire future employees. Going through day to day, working, going to school, and life as normal, we received our approval letter from the State to become an enrolled provider through the State of North Carolina. We were so excited and things were looking up. This was our first milestone as partners. We had achieved some of our goals. Next, we had to determine where our first client would come from. About two months went by, anxiously waiting, and I received a call on my personal cell phone. It was a sunny day in the afternoon. I was just getting out of my multicultural counseling class, and walking to my car when my phone rang, and I answered. The caller stated that she had a lady who was experiencing some depressive symptoms and needed to have an intake and clinical assessment for services. I smiled, was excited, and gathered information over the phone to meet the client to schedule our first appointment. When the call ended, I immediately called my partner and shared the good news, jumping up and down that we just received our first referral. We both went the client's home together to complete the intake.

As a result, from our first referral, we were able to start providing clinical services. Since my partners and I all had bachelor's degrees in the industry of our work, we didn't have to hire additional people. My partners and I decided to split the hours and work with the client while managing the business operations as well. From there, our work started to speak for itself and the three of us were known as "The Girls". We shared classes together, we went to provider forums together, and we spent a lot of time together. We all passionately grew and developed our business as this would be our livelihood. We positioned ourselves to earn six figures.

Throughout the years, we all grew and developed personally and professionally at different rates. We hired and trained staff to work in programs in the community. Eventually, we developed into women who had gained confidence, skills, and expertise. In early 2009, I started to feel detach between my partners. I felt I didn't belong there. There was confrontation, strife, and mismanagement of funds, but I promised myself I would work through it because I was a partner invested into what I started. In the meantime, I was reconnected to someone who I had known as a child. In my younger years, I was his girlfriend. We re-developed our friendship, starting dating, and grew fond of each other. In our conversations, we talked about our interests, values, and goals for life. We dated and discovered a powerful energy between us. He allowed me to be authentic. I shared with him my feelings about my career and that I felt disconnected to something I had helped create. I thought it was time to leave, but didn't know how. I had nothing to go to. After dating, eventually, he proposed in the summer of 2009, and we married the same year. Everything seemed to happen so fast, but I knew in my heart it was right.

In June 2009, I remember attending a service in Raleigh, North

Carolina and that night, my pastor, Dr. Kevin A. Williams, spoke over my life. He stated, "Your business is going to be blessed, you will become a millionaire, your accounts will have so much money you are going to ask yourself how I got here. I need you to write down five locations where you want your business to be located, and tell your future husband he has a good woman." I was amazed at what I had been told and wrote down the locations thinking how to get in five locations because that was not in my plan. I received the word and held it close to my heart daily.

> *We experienced a lifestyle and MINDSET change. Our faith was increased and the UNITY of our bond strengthened.*

My life had just experienced a major transition. I was delighted at where my life was headed. After discussions with my husband, and explaining how I felt about my current career situation, we consulted God, our Pastor, and decided to start our own private agency. I submitted my resignation to the company in November 2009 and agreed to work until December 31, 2009 to transition and close out things.

Well, I was told by my partners that December 7, 2009 would be my last day. Immediately, after I submitted my resignation, my partners that I loved, who were my friends, whom I spent many holidays and family gatherings with, had become my enemies. I experienced so many emotions; I was sad, lonely, overwhelmed, hurt, and curious as to why I was treated in such a hostile way. I dreaded going into the office during my last month because it was a tense and hostile environment. I cried by myself and to my husband, and felt so rejected by my partners and staff. I was expecting a financial buy out from my company so we would have money to live off throughout the launch of our new business.

However, I was told by my partners and accounting firm the company didn't have any money, and in fact, I would have liabilities. I left the company only with a cell phone that they disconnected shortly after and a laptop. In spite of lost friendships and relationships, being gossiped about, and a loss of a thriving income, my husband and I were able to withstand the storm and test. It was not easy at all, as a matter of fact, it was challenging on our novel marriage. As my life transitioned, first there was marriage, second the resignation from a company where I was a partner, then launch a new business with my husband; it all seemed so chaotic.

Thankfully, we both were paid well before marriage and we were able to have a savings. Well, with our savings of $12,500 and with some help from our families, we got through the next four months of our lives. Those four months were a faith walk for us. We experienced a lifestyle and mindset change. Our faith was increased and the unity of our bond strengthened. Things that were a luxury to us we could no longer afford. We packed peanut butter and jelly sandwiches and shared a bag of chips for lunch several days. Out of our savings, we decided to invest $1,545 in our new business, Wrights Care Services, LLC, in Greensboro, N.C., which was for a single office space which included insurance, a computer, and a business license. Simultaneously, I worked three contract jobs as a therapist and my husband worked two jobs, while we both worked on developing our new private, behavioral health company. We submitted our application and policies to the state in late 2009 to become a provider. Our household income went from about $7,500 a month to $2,500 a month. Even though we had a significant decrease in our income, we remained faithful to God in paying our tithes and offerings.

This was a different phase for me. My husband and I started from scratch to build our legacy. We depleted all of our accounts including our IRAs to keep everything together. In developing our behavioral health agency in North Carolina, we knew leaders and owners would need certain credentials and knowledge in order to thrive as an agency. Since I received my Master of Science in Rehabilitation Counseling, it prepared me to pursue licensure as a professional counselor. Therefore, in late 2009, with all of the chaos going on, I started that process and became a Licensed Professional Counselor Associate. This allowed me to provide counseling services to families, individuals, and children and conduct clinical assessments while being supervised by a licensed professional. This additional credential allowed me to develop skills while earning additional income.

> In order to be successful in *life,* I had to **FAIL, MAKE MISTAKES,** develop, *grow,* and *learn.*

While waiting for our approval letter from the state, we continued to balance and juggle family and several jobs, while all remaining faithful to paying our tithes. We prayed together and stayed up countless nights and hours developing policies and program material to launch our agency. There were times I wanted to quit and give up, but I knew my life had a purpose to genuinely help people. Times were difficult and very overwhelming. To get through some of those tough times I prayed, meditated, read self-help and inspirational books, wrote goals down, and set benchmarks.

After months of waiting, we finally received our letter from the state of North Carolina in March 2010 to provide two services to children and adults. In the beginning, my husband and I were able to work in those programs without hiring too many additional staff. I was overjoyed we had received the letter to provide services. It came just on time. It was our breakthrough and our lives would change forever. Six months prior, my life was in a drought, I experienced rejection, loneliness, loss of friends, and fear. With support from my husband, family, and a few close friends, I was able to find my peace and happiness again.

In the development of Wrights Care Services, I knew operational systems had to be in place, a strategic business plan had to be created, and individuals had to be hired in areas we were weak in. I knew I couldn't be afraid to ask for help if I didn't know something. Our first year in business was challenging and overwhelming. There were several state mandates that had to be met which tripled our payroll. With that known, we lost money and found it difficult to be financially viable. We asked ourselves should we quit before we get too far or brainstorm ways to make our agency viable and profitable.

We planned and offered additional services based on what the community needed, and we partnered and collaborated with other organizations. In addition, throughout the years, we opened an office in another state and three rural cities in North Carolina. I, alongside with my husband, has worked very hard to build Wrights Care Services and develop a reputation and creditability in the community and state. There were times I was petrified of making the same mistakes from my previous business such as not communicating effectively and experiencing growth at a rapid rate and not developing operational systems. From my first business mistakes, I was able to truly learn what not to do in the next. I know that may sound like a cliché, but in order to be successful in life, I had to fail, make mistakes, develop, grow, and learn.

Above all, as a wife, mother, and entrepreneur, I have learned how to trust God, be patient, faithful, forgiving, confident, skilled, and balanced. There is not a single formula to growth, development, and success, but a fusion of vision, dedication, risks, failures, and successes. I have experienced balancing family, career, and life to be rewarding and challenging at the same time. From the growth of one business, I was able to expand to other profitable ventures and become diversified in various industries and with income. It did not happen overnight, but with vision, dedication, and tenacity, I was able to diversify.

It is critical to have a support system and team who wants to see you succeed, develop, and grow. Being surrounded with positive, driven, and purpose-filled individuals aided me in my journey to success. I have committed myself to continued learning, discipline, and purpose. When I get exhausted, I take time to relax, refocus and think. I would encourage you to go through a journey of self-discovery: have vision, set goals, develop benchmarks, and when you achieve those, celebrate the accomplishments and successes and learn from the failures. From all of my experiences, I am a true believer that my determination and faith in God have led to my success. I could have allowed my academic and business failure, and other disappointments stop me from transforming into the purpose-filled woman that I am. I hope you, too, can find a place through the pain, rejection, or distress to flourish past your failure.

Evangelist Tequita C. Brice
Author: The Mandate of a Virtuous Woman

Evangelist Tequita C. Brice is the founder of Virtuous Woman Ministries of North Carolina, Inc., a women's ministry dedicated to building, strengthening, and empowering women through the study and practical life application of God's Word. Tequita's ministry is grounded in and fueled by her foundational scripture, St. John 4:34, for her utmost desire is sincerely to please God. You may reach Evangelist Brice on the web at: virtuouswomanministriesnc.org or by calling 336.612.1392.

STORY 3

The Mandate of a Virtuous Woman

For so long, I wrestled with the feeling that the *"Proverbs 31 woman"* was someone not real or literal. She was an icon, a symbol; she was someone for me to pattern myself after and a goal to strive to reach. A product of misinformation, virtuous to me meant that I had to be perfect and no matter how hard I tried, I knew perfection would never be attained. It wasn't until God needed me to see the value in who I was as a woman—called to His work when man tried to "strip me" of the purpose ordained for my life—that I gained an understanding of this extraordinary woman.

I was born into a legacy of preachers so I guess you could say my calling was inevitable...or maybe not. Trust me; I didn't get it by process of osmosis. Just as David was anointed and sent back to the field to continue to be "processed"[1], I had to be tried and found worthy to be bestowed with the anointing that one needs to carry out the call, and this is where my story begins.

My mother was an anointed psalmist and my father was a gifted musician. Some would consider this a formula for greatness. My father's side gave me the gift of music and my mother's side laid the foundation for everything else that was Holy and Godly in my life. My mother's father was the Vice Bishop of a large Pentecostal Holiness organization and my father's father was a United Holiness Church Pastor.

I grew up singing in the church and matriculated in music ministry. I loved singing so much, I secretly dreamed of a career in the music industry. My influences were the likes of the Clark Sisters, Vanessa Bell Armstrong, Whitney Houston and Anita Baker. I began singing in talent shows in school in fifth grade and was always commended for my talent. However, at age twelve, my interests began to change. My father had begun to exhibit relational inconsistencies in my life which left a huge void. Suddenly boys became a priority in my life and everything else was secondary. I was your typical teenager but with one exception: I just wanted to be loved.

I developed a relationship with God at an early age and with that relationship formed a desire in me to please God. At age thirteen, I watched a science-fiction movie entitled Dune.[2] For reasons that I couldn't explain, there was so much biblical parallelism in the movie for me. The main character had a purpose to lead a people to true freedom, but he wasn't sure that he was the Kwisatz Haderach that had been foretold. There was a phrase that was repeated in the movie: the sleeper must awaken. For whatever reason, this phrase spoke to me and I wrote it down. I had no idea that it was to be the title of my initial sermon, but I tucked it away in my Bible and pondered its meaning everyday confident that God would reveal its purpose in due time. I just knew that there was something greater for me to do in God's kingdom, and I would embrace it with fervor because of my love for Christ. My problem was that the enemy, too, had gotten wind of this information and he set about a plan for my demise.

Lack of fathering and continuous parental abandonment forced me to desire male companionship much sooner than I was able to handle the pressure that came along with it, which kept my focus compromised. My parents also made a fatal decision to move to my father's hometown. Now I was miles away from my weekly routine of church twice a week and the accountability that my grandparents provided for me and was left to my own devices. With my focus now compromised, this idle time allowed me to be negatively influenced into dropping my standards, and the summer before I was due to begin high school, I lost my virginity.

The few times the topic of sex was brought up in our household, my mother threatened that she would know when or if it happened to me. I wasn't sure if she knew, but she never addressed me about it. In my naiveté, I took that to mean I was safe. Now the enemy had me compromising the Word of God in my life. Not only did I know pre-marital sex was wrong, once I'd opened the door for my flesh to be satisfied in that way, I couldn't convince myself that it hadn't happened. I thought I'd gotten away with it so I allowed it to continue. But the bond I had formed with sin created within me a false sense of security. Romans 6: 1-2 (AMP) says,

> *So what do we do? Keep on sinning so God can keep on forgiving? I should hope not! If we've left the country where sin is sovereign, how can we still live in our old house there? Or didn't you realize we packed up and left there for good?*

I got comfortable and careless and a year later, I was pregnant. I knew it the moment it happened. I wasn't using any birth control so I had gotten very good at managing my menstrual cycle, i.e., when I was ovulating and when I was in the most danger for conception (so I thought). A week later, my cycle didn't come. I panicked. However, being that I had never been this late before, I already suspected the worst. I couldn't ask my parents for money without an explanation as to what it was for so I saved my lunch money for a week and bought a pregnancy test. The plus sign confirmed my suspicions and left me utterly distraught. What have I done! I immediately was in a state of fear. I was so sorry for what I had done, but what I feared more was the thought of having to tell my parents.

Growing up, I had heard horror stories about my other family members who had gotten pregnant who had to endure public humiliation by standing in front of the church, confessing their sin of fornication, and asking for forgiveness because of the fact that they were now pregnant. The experience was completely devastating for the mother to be, and I knew I didn't have the fortitude to endure something like that. In my mind, it was nothing short of a public execution! I had always been shy and quiet, the perfect child (in my mind at least), miss goodie two shoes. I was the child that you only had to talk to and I would cry as if I'd had a switch taken to me. This could not happen to me.

The box stated that the test was 99% accurate, but I wasn't convinced. The test had to be wrong. I tried to reason with myself. I recalled stories of other girls in school I'd heard had my issue. The very idea of the shame and scrutiny I would have to endure was too much for me to fathom. So, I made an appointment at the health department. When the nurse returned with the results, I sat there in shock. I could no longer ignore the truth. A million questions ran through my mind. How would I take care of it? Would my parents let me stay once they found out or would they kick me out? The more questions I conjured up, the more I realized the magnitude of what was happening to me and the more afraid I became. All I knew was that I couldn't tell my family. So I carried a secret shame.

For weeks, I carried my secret shame but fear of the unknown was literally driving me insane. I had to get some closure to this situation. Against my better judgment, I decided to have an abortion.

The morning of the procedure, I was dropped off at the clinic and waited for what seemed like hours. I had to watch a film about conception and what happens to the fetus during the process. I was horrified of what was about to take place, but I was even more horrified at the thought of everyone finding out. So I stayed. But there was a problem. The nurse called me out of the room back to the lobby. My boyfriend who'd dropped me off hours earlier to meet his father to get the money for the procedure had returned without the money. It seemed that his grandmother had intercepted the money and she refused to relinquish it without an explanation.

Great! The last thing I wanted to do was to give an explanation. Once we understood though that we weren't going to get the money otherwise, no problem—we thought. We'd just go tell her. We thought offering her some further clarification would be simple enough and we could just turn around and go back. We were wrong.

Nervously, I pleaded my case to this woman of wisdom as to why I could not have this child. I explained how it would devastate my family and basically make me an outcast for life. Yes, I may have exaggerated the outcast for life; however, I was very afraid of the blemish it would leave. I had magnified the negatives of bringing a child into the world under these circumstances so much that I almost hyperventilated at the table. However, despite all of my pleading, the grandmother refused to give us the money. While she stated she was sympathetic to my plight, her concern was that if something were to go wrong while I was on that table, no one from my family would be aware. She didn't want the responsibility of having to be the one to explain. I understood what she was saying, but it was not what I wanted, and I was even more devastated. Determined not to be deterred, I begged my boyfriend to ask his father for more money. When that didn't happen, I begged him to get a job; I begged him to just do something.

For weeks, I waited for him to find a way to raise the capital we needed. Helpless, I finally gave in to the notion that I was going to have to have the child. Still trying to do as much damage control as possible, I resolved to not tell my parents but to let them find out on their own. I figured once I began to show, it would be too late for them to do anything about it.

I wore big clothes to hide my predicament. However, it was much more difficult than I expected to conceal the seed that was growing inside me. I was always sleepy and beginning to experience the changes a woman's body goes through when she's with child.

Then came the dreadful night of trust gone bad. I could no longer keep my pregnancy a secret. I felt I had to tell somebody. I told my girlfriends at school and asked them not to tell anyone. One night at church, I told my cousin. She had experienced this so I thought she was a "safe person" to confide in. I'd felt so alone through the entire process. I just wanted someone to comfort me and tell me that everything was going to be alright. For whatever reason, she thought differently. I know she thought she was helping me, but she betrayed my trust and told her mother, my aunt, who in turn told my mother.

After church that night, my mother sent my sister and I home with my father and stayed behind to talk to my aunt. She never did that because she knew we didn't like riding with him. So for her to not allow us to stay behind with her, we knew something was wrong. And knowing that I had just revealed my secret shame, I knew her sending us ahead was not coincidental. I had a sinking feeling I was about to be exposed.

Sure enough, as soon as my mother got home, she walked up the stairs and called for me. As I moved towards the door, my legs felt like lead as I stumbled from my room to the hallway. There was no way of escape for me now. There, in front of my father, she asked me if I was pregnant. Terrified, I stood there in front of them both and lied to their faces. She was so angry she could barely look at me. She told my father that she had just had the most humiliating conversation with her sister and her mother about what I'd revealed to my cousin only hours before.

Finally, I had to come clean and admit not just the pregnancy but the fact that I had tried to handle the situation on my own for fear of this very moment. I told them that I had gone to have an abortion but that my boyfriend's grandmother refused to give us the money. I tried to convey to them that she didn't want the responsibility falling solely on her if anything went wrong. At that moment, my mother was too overcome with emotion to continue the conversation. Tears ran down her face and she excused herself to her room. "I… I'm sorry." I tried to say it, but the words seemed to lodge themselves in the middle of my throat refusing to come out. I lay in bed that night and cried myself to sleep. I was sure when morning arrived, I would learn my fate.

The next morning I was forced to call my boyfriend and let him know that our secret was out. I told him that my parents had found out about the pregnancy and that they decided it was in the best interests of all involved to proceed with the abortion. My father stopped by the grandmother's house on the way to the clinic to pick up the money. I was overwhelmed with so many emotions. Mostly, I was embarrassed, not so much because they knew I was pregnant, but because my pregnancy meant that I was sexually active. The shame that overtook me put me in an immediate state of depression. My mother left out that morning and wouldn't even look at me. I was crushed. The one person I needed the most wouldn't help me.

Once I arrived at the clinic, they remembered me from my previous visit. Even though I had already seen the video, it was procedure that I sit through it again. This time, though, I sat through it in tears. The nurse gave me tissue and asked if I was sure I wanted to go through with it. I told her I had no choice.

After the procedure was over, I sat in the recovery room for about an hour. My father was there to take me home. We didn't speak but the silence in the car all the way home was deafening. He stopped at the drug store to fill the prescription for pain pills the clinic gave me. Then I returned home and lay in bed waiting for the pain medicine to kick in. The pain was so intense that I cried out, but there was no one there to soothe me, no one to hold me and tell me that everything was going to be alright. Somehow I had crossed over this imaginary line into a place I should not have been. I'd made an adult decision to engage in sexual activity and I was far too young to understand the consequences of my actions.

I was angry for allowing myself to be in this predicament. I had waited so long to have the abortion; I had gotten used to the life living inside me. Now that this choice had been made for me, I felt that I was somehow exiled from God. After all, didn't he command, "Thou shalt not kill"?[3] But the damage had been done, and I was left to figure out how to put the pieces back together, alone. I prayed that God would forgive me for my sins and not hold this grave injustice against me. I prayed that I was not out of His will. I prayed… eventually exhausted, I fell to sleep and slept the remainder of the day.

Some hours later, my father woke me up to tell me I had a phone call. It was my grandmother. She was calling to check on me, but I was too ashamed to speak. My father put the phone up to my ear. She told me that I didn't have to talk; I could just listen. I still remember her kind words, "I know you're probably not feeling your best, but I just wanted you to know that I love you and that you're still my sweet girl." That's what she always called me, her sweet girl. It was too much for me to hear at that moment. I burst into tears and my father pulled the phone away. I didn't feel sweet. As a matter of fact, I felt worthless, and there was no one there telling me anything to the contrary. I could hear her tell him that she didn't mean to upset me. He told her that I would be alright and that he would have my mother call her when she got home from work.

When my mother returned home, she reiterated how disappointed she was in me. She said that I had broken her trust and that it would take a long time for me to gain it back. Her words stung like lashes from a whip. I was grounded indefinitely at that point which included no phone calls and no extracurricular activities. I was to go to school only and back home again. I could tell my mother was deeply hurt by the entire situation, but she chose to close herself off from me instead of embracing me and allowing us to heal together.

Once I returned to school, I told my best friends what happened. They were sorry that I'd had to experience such pain. I hadn't told anyone else but them; however, that afternoon, I was called to my cheerleading coach's office. Just when I needed healing and consolation from my traumatic ordeal, she ripped what scab had begun to form completely off and told me that I was benched for the remainder of the season. What was worse, I had to report to practices and games as normal, but I would not be allowed to participate. Although I thought I had handled my situation in secret, I had not escaped the public humiliation I feared so much. So, in addition to my private hell, I had to endure being publicly ridiculed weekly as people behind me whispered why I had been benched. Like Hester Prynne[4], I felt as though attached to my bosom was a large red felt "A" for abortion. I felt despised and rejected, but there was no consolation for me. And the mental and emotional weight of it all caused me to want to do nothing more than to retreat into my own private shell.

Somehow, I managed to make it through the rest of the school year. However, before I could get excited, my mother informed me that she was shipping me off to New York to stay with my uncle and aunt for the summer. They had just had their first child and she thought it was befitting that I get hands on experience helping to care for a newborn since I thought I was so ready. I was shattered. In my selfish thinking, I thought, how will my relationship ever survive with me that far away for the whole summer? I felt she was being quite unfair to say the least. But I would have; I was only sixteen.

Before I could say my goodbyes, I was whisked off five states away from home for the entire summer. Despite my initial feelings that I had just been sentenced to life in prison, my uncle and aunt were very kind to me. However, they were clear that my job was to take care of my newborn cousin during the day while they were working. My aunt had just gone back to work part-time, but the hours she was gone felt like years. I had a crash course in holding, feeding, changing, and putting a baby boy to sleep. I was constantly terrified of doing something wrong.

My uncle and aunt showered me with love as best as they could. They always spoke kindly to me and allowed me to speak freely. I could tell the subject of my pregnancy had stirred up quite the controversy in my family, but as with most things, no one discussed it. It was brushed under the proverbial family rug like it never happened. My uncle had weekly heart to heart talks with me about my feelings and why I thought I'd ended up this way. It was hard to discuss, but he knew that my parents' volatile relationship probably had something to do with it. He did very well in choosing his words so as not to hurt my feelings.

> My MANDATE to be
> a *Virtuous Woman*
> *had not so much to do with*
> MY LINEAGE as with
> *God's* ORIGINAL
> INTENT *for my life*
> *was planned*
> *before I was even born.*

The conversations proved to be very cathartic for me. I was able to convey to him that I felt like I was grown up enough to handle my life. After all, I had been making my own decisions for years. Illusioned, I had convinced myself that I could make life work and live happily ever after when, in fact, I was still nothing more than an impressionable child. I was socially age appropriate, but emotionally, I was still that little girl who wanted nothing more than her parents love, attention, and approval.

My uncle took those few weeks and helped me "get my head back on straight". He reminded me of who I was—my purpose and the potential I possessed to acquire everything that God had in store for me. He was my mother's advocate in explaining that she was so hurt because she saw herself in me and she didn't want me to repeat the same mistakes she made. Although my parents were married when I was born, they married young (my mother was 16 and my father was 19) …too young to understand that it takes two mature adults to have a successful marriage and raise children.

Armed with my new reality, I returned to North Carolina at the end of the summer, but I was different. Not only had I been changed by what I just survived, but now my purpose and reason for being was reignited. I concentrated on completing my last two years of school and moving on to college. I was successful in turning my life around and learned some valuable lessons in the process. I learned that it was my mandate to be a virtuous woman and it had not so much to do with my lineage as with what God's original intent for my life was before I was even born. But I had to find this out for myself.

I'd been tricked into believing my value was wrapped up in what I could give to people and not in just who God made me. And I had fallen

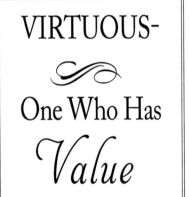

VIRTUOUS-

One Who Has

Value

into the trap of trying to prove to people that I was worth so much more than what they saw. Even though I had been called, I was afraid that because of my past, I would not be accepted. I was afraid of being judged for the decisions I made during my era of misunderstanding. Nevertheless, I had to relinquish the debilitating fear that kept me from moving forward. Second Timothy 1:7(AMP) says,

For God did not give us a spirit of timidity (of cowardice, of craven and cringing and fawning fear), but [He has given us a spirit] of power and of love and of calm and well-balanced mind and discipline and self-control.

Most of us are aware that anxiety, terror, and panic are not from God, but we often fail to put emotions like timidity and worry in the same category. Shyness and timidity is the fear of what others think of us. Once I became secure in the fact that God loved me no matter what, I understood that I did not have to fear any man. Gradually, my shyness and timidity was replaced with confidence and boldness. Proverbs 29:25(NIV) says, *"Fear of man will prove to be a snare, but whoever trusts in the Lord is kept safe."* I needed to understand love but not just any love, the perfect love of God.

The Proverbs 31:10-31 scripture has been the subject of many a Mother's Day messages; however, it was what God wanted me to know about what defined a virtuous woman that turned my life around. The word "virtuous" comes from the Hebrew word chayil[5] meaning a force, means or other resources; wealth, virtue, valor, strength, able, might, power, riches, and worth. These words together represent someone that has value. This was especially important for me as I didn't understand my value in God's eyes. I allowed my circumstances to convince me that I somehow wasn't good enough. This, in turn, caused me to develop an unhealthy need to please. It was in pleasing people that I felt validated, when in reality, I never had to do anything; God said I was valuable just the way I was.

So, it was with my new found understanding of whom I was and my purpose that I was able to finally accept the call to ministry in July 1996. And I've never looked back.

ENDNOTES

1. 1 Samuel 17
2. Dune (1984). [film] David Lynch.
3. Exodus 20:13
4. Hawthorne, N. (1900). The Scarlet Letter. Boston [U.S.A.]: Houghton Mifflin [U.A.].
5. Brown, Driver, Briggs and Gesenius. "Hebrew Lexicon entry for Chayil". "The NAS Old Testament Hebrew Lexicon".

Rev. Stephanie M. Graham
Author: Scarred Tissue

Rev. Stephanie M. Graham resides in Baltimore, Maryland with her two daughters, Sequoya, 23 and Aaronica, 15. A veteran of the United States Navy, she has a B.S. in Business Communications and is pursuing her Master's of Divinity at Howard University School of Divinity. She is the founder of two ministries, The Gratefulness Project and the Righteous Readers Book Club. She has published her first book, "I Am Just a Voice," a compilation of sermons and reflections. Her second book, "Worshipping through the Wounds" will be published in the fall of 2013. You can reach Rev. Graham by email at smariegraham@gmail.com or by phone at 410-504-7626.

STORY 4

Scarred Tissue

Too dark at birth, not the preferred one, looking for a lighter complexion baby…well, I was the only black baby born that night, so you had to take me home. Felt like a consolation prize, a token, so while you kept searching for the one you really wanted, I began searching too. Searching for the real me wherever she could be. I searched in people, places and things. I never could identify with why I was, the way I was, and even now I ask why I am who I am. Does anybody even notice me? I never seemed to fit in, grew up distracted by the shade of my skin, always feeling like the darker child, the black one. Look at me now! You can't see what my life has become. I work wonders with a pen, but at the end of the day, I still remember where my story begins. I was never good enough, not even for you. How could you expect anyone else to see the real me, that you couldn't even see? Didn't my smile win your heart? My words and utterances spoke volumes from the start. Everyone thought I was going somewhere, even I thought my life would have meaning, yet all the time my heart was screaming-SCREAMING! Can't you see me; am I worth a second look or do I need to pour it all out on the pages of a book? Will I have a chance to make you take a second glance? Will I ever be good enough? In this life, I've only one story to tell; it's mine, not yours. The truth is I see how much you long to be a part of me. Low self-worth, I bid you farewell. Tonight I lie down with you, but tomorrow I will get up as a new me!

SCAR TISSUE doesn't REMAIN *hidden*.

Born with an issue of blood, I was broken at an early age by the color of my skin. The infraction, disregard, and rejection did not come from outside my race, but inside my family. The outside world had not yet discovered the scars that were forming a few hours after my birth. There were so many issues that existed before I was even born, it was almost certain I would be born with scarred tissue. My birth would be God's way of unraveling the ball of confusion and tangled web of insecurity, rejection, bitterness, and deep seeds of pain in my family.

We go on day after day, month after month, year after year, pretending we are just fine, our families are fine, our children will be fine, and our family isn't any different than any other family. I'm so sick of the phrase,: "All families have some dysfunction." Does that somehow justify the hurt we inflict upon the ones we love? Your child could be broken today. Your sister could hate you and not know why. You can't seem to understand why your grandmother and your aunt haven't spoken in years. There is no excuse for the anguish family members suffer. The Bible declares that God sent His Son that we might have life more abundantly (see John 10:10)! Abundance means great quantity, well supplied, over sufficient. To live any other way is to be deficient and beneath your inheritance.

Yet, life for me appeared to be normal. Nobody could see what I was going through and everyone assumed I was just like every other little girl. Except the truth is, scar tissue doesn't remain hidden. It's tissue that appears after an injury. It's impossible to remove the scar tissue because there will always be damage to the tissue even after it has healed. The infraction is a reminder of the cut. Like a physical scar that interrupts the smoothness of your skin, a deep seeded emotional scar normally doesn't bother you unless you bother it. So, I made certain not to touch it and kept moving through my life with a smile on my face. I became a rising star in my family while all of the time feeling like the black sheep. What an oxymoron using black and star to describe the same person.

From the looks of things, I had everything going for me. I was the first baby born in the family. I grew up with a host of older cousins that loved me like I was their baby, long before any of them had children of their own. Then their children grew to love me like a big sister. Life was grand as far as I could see…this may be when I first noticed the scarring. You see scarred tissue is the result of connective tissue that forms over a healed wound or cut. I admit that there was some connective tissue that covered a wound I had refused to acknowledge and began to disentangle itself as my teenage years began.

In an effort to mask the pain, I found solace in extracurricular activities. Who knew that there was anything hidden under the surface. I seemed happy and content in the skin that I was in. But in fact, it was this very skin that brought me such pain. Day after day, all anyone could see was the brown face that smiled and danced and danced and smiled. The little girl, who sang in the choir, had lots of friends and was the center of so much attention and affection. All the while, she was feeling alone in a room full of people. Since I didn't know the root or cause of the pain, I had no idea of what to do with it, so I ignored it. The little girl became a young woman, and the scar began to bleed, and eventually, the pain intensified and the wound became deeper and deeper, deeper than words could express.

By the time I entered 10th grade, I began looking for love, acceptance, and validation to define my worth. It wasn't enough that I had danced on various stages, performed plays around the city, had the love and admiration of my family, and was the highlight of my house…there was an emptiness under the scar that no one saw. Thus, when the acceptance and validation came from an unlikely candidate, another teenager with problems of his own, we seemed like perfection. The outward appearance that he could represent as the perfect salve for my scar couldn't have been farther from the truth. Nothing could be farther from the truth. While it seemed that he was silencing the voices that told me "I wasn't good enough, I was too dark, my dreams were too big and that I was unlovable", he was actually making me the object of his rule and dominion. Instead of affirming me, he controlled me; instead of loving me, he used me; instead of building me up, he helped to tear me down…and I truly loved him. I gave him the only innocence that I had left, and he didn't deserve it and so, he misused it and abused it.

For the first time in my life, I understood what it meant to be in bondage and held captive. I became a slave to a young man who lived in my neighborhood and was supposed to care about me. I did things for him that I never imagined that I would do. I had sold my soul to the devil and I didn't even want it back. I liked being used, abused, and cursed out, in private and in public. What should have been considered embarrassment was for me the result of his affection. I was starving for attention and he gave it to me. Not once during this three year period did I ever think that I was worth more, deserved more, and desired more. All I wanted was more of him.

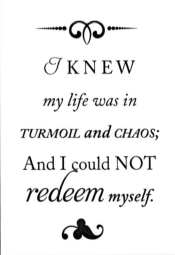

I KNEW

my life was in

TURMOIL and CHAOS;

And I could NOT

redeem myself.

Until the day that he did to me what I was all too familiar with from my childhood…he rejected me. This rejection became the puncture wound that would cause more bleeding. This agitation to my scarred tissue left me in a state of emergency and I needed immediate assistance to recover. My heart was broken, my spirit was crushed, my body was worn-out, and I was bent over at 17. It was October 19, 1986, in my senior year in high school, that I sought the Lord for myself and gave my life to Christ. This was a quite unusual event because I was a member of a Catholic church all of my childhood. I had no understanding of salvation at that time, but I knew my life was in turmoil and chaos, and I could not redeem myself. There had to be someone who could help me gain the strength to fight for my life, my worth, and my dignity. It couldn't be my mother because I wasn't so sure that she could love me past all of the things that I had done. I had no idea who could accept me and the actions that I had played out and the foolish life I had led and still love me. But I heard a voice from heaven in a song, "If you confess the Lord, call Him up, if you believe in the Father, the Son and the Holy Ghost, call Him up and tell Him what you want" and that ushered me into the presence of a loving, forgiving, redeeming, nurturing God who I had only prayed to up to this point, but had no real relationship with. This moment was a defining one in my life. It was the starting line for a new beginning, but there would be much work to do.

When I think back on my life at this time, I am reminded of a scene in the movie, Things We Lost in the Fire. There was a list that had to be written of all of the things that were lost. Of all the things that I lost in that relationship, I have to remember as Fantasia sings, "sometimes we have to lose to win." I won Jesus and in the journey, I reflect on the hurts, pains, anguish, and suffering that led me to restoration, and in that process, I found joy. Why does it hurt so badly? If it didn't hurt, you wouldn't have looked to God for comfort. If it didn't hurt so badly, you might make the mistake of touching it again, wanting it again, and hanging around for more hurt. If it didn't hurt so badly, you would have never learned the lesson that everything that is good to you is not good for you. If it didn't hurt so badly, how would you have moved from hurt to healing? How would you share your testimony of how you got over? If it didn't hurt so badly, you wouldn't know what it means to have loved and lost only to gain unconditional love. So you ask, why does it hurt so badly, and I answer, just because it does. It's time to take your hurts and find wholeness. Take your hurts and move towards healing. Take your hurts and find peace. Take your hurts and find Him. He is waiting for you with His arms wide open. Find safety and refuge in the arms of Jesus. Why does it hurt so badly?

I REFLECT *on the hurts, pains, anguish, and suffering that led me to* RESTORATION, *and in that process,* I FOUND *joy.*

It doesn't hurt anymore like it used to, but now it helps me to help others who hurt like I once hurt. It doesn't hurt too long even when it hurts so badly. The verdict was in, I made the decision to move on and never look back. I would get as far away from my past as I could. I would get caught up in the wind and be free.

The time came to change the scenery and my path in life. In 1989, I joined the United States Navy, a whole new world. Things would be unlike I had ever imagined. My journey took me to the West Coast and dropped me in the middle of a strange land with a diverse group of people. I was a young woman with wings, to fly, soar, and be free. I was accountable to nobody but myself and my superior officers, of course. I started to put the pieces of my broken heart back together and was living my life like it was golden. Well, how many of you know, we can all talk a good game until it's time to be tested. I felt like I was my best self, until I met a young Marine who caught my attention. You see, I was over my past hurts and I knew the Lord pretty well, so I thought, until I was faced with the reality of who I was. The truth is I was still broken, empty, and confused about who I truly was. Up under this tough exterior that the Navy had molded and shaped to make me the Security Officer that I was, there was still a little girl who looked in the mirror and saw she still wasn't good enough. This allowed me to fall prey to any man who could woo me into his arms by simply saying what I needed to hear. I still had a strong desire to be accepted, affirmed, and worthy of a man's affection and his attention.

In no time, I found myself carrying this man's child and bringing my military career to a close, choosing "parenthood" over service to my country. Don't get me wrong; it was the right decision for me at the time, but my mother always said, "Hind sight is 20/20." I should have made some other decisions. Since I knew what it felt like to grow up without a father in the house, I would not tolerate this for my precious daughter. I married my daughter's father without reservation. She would have the benefit of having a two parent household even if it destroyed me…and that's exactly what it did! I was miserable, manic, and manipulative. I became bitter and bound. It was a hostile environment, and I pretended that everything was fine. All the while, I was raising my daughter in the midst of my pain and suffocating her with the deficiency of my own low self-esteem. It's funny how people see only what we want them to see, not once did anyone pry into the affairs of my life, or peer into the window of my heart, or even scratch the surface of my well put together foundation to see that I was moving, breathing, living behind a wall, wearing a mask, and hiding the scars. I was sleeping with the enemy and it was the inner-me that was being silenced and dying on the vine. I could barely stand the sight of my own face. My joy was not complete and my happiness was borrowed. Everything about my life was a lie! It was a façade and I played the part in excellence. Sounds a lot like the teenage girl who had run from this very same life only five years ago, and here I was at 23-years-old, living the life of dysfunction and pandemonium. How could my daughter be a healthy child in the center of such heartache? I shielded her as much as I could. I created for her a sanctuary of peace, love, and joy even when I knew none for myself.

This is the time when some would go crazy, lose their sanity and their minds; start drinking, start smoking, and gambling their futures away. I could have taken any of those paths, but I decided to get even! Getting even is never a good path to embark upon. It can lead you to destruction, desperation, and even death. I chose to take on the characteristics of everyone who had rejected, betrayed, and mistreated me. If becoming them would settle the score and even out the playing field, then I was all for it. Paul said in Romans, that the good I want to do, I do not do (Romans 7:18-23). I became the very thing that I despised, the one who rejects. I got involved with men who I had no intentions of being in real relationship with. I deliberately used them, called on them for favors, played the part but carried myself as the object of desire only to cut it off, drop them, and walk away at a moment's notice. I felt like it was time they knew what it felt like to be wanted and used, rejected and discarded, played with like a game. It was my turn to call the shots, but I still felt alone, empty, and bitter. All this took place during my separation. After five years of marriage, I filed for divorce and moved on once again.

By now, I had nothing left to give; I was depleted. There is a song about it…"They say I am hopeless, as a penny with a hole in it" (Dionne Farris was singing my mantra). Moving on was becoming more and more difficult with each agitation to my scarred tissue. I never seemed to be in the healing process long enough to get a scab over the infected area. Before you know it, I was back in the mix trying to fix what I could not. At this point in time, I needed to hear a song, a word, a poem, a bird chirping, or even read a billboard that would bring me back to myself. I was like a ship without a sail, lost at sea, numb to the breeze, and oblivious to the voice or presence of God. Some would equate my existence to that of a functional alcoholic; I was moving through time and space without any direction, purpose or destination in sight. Yet still, no one knew…but God. In my mind, I began to wonder, if God knew, why hadn't He done something. Or had He done something and I was completely unaware of what had taken place. It's now 1996 and while it's only been 27 years since my arrival, I feel like I have lived 50 years of a hard life. This sentence has been excruciating and debilitating to say the least. Who knew that it would be this difficult getting to 30?

As if my own hurts, inadequacies and shortcomings weren't enough, I began to notice brokenness in my daughter. She still had a smile, her laughter still brought joy to my ears, and we shared a passion and bond for each other that were unbreakable. But I found a letter she had scribbled on a piece of paper when she was in the 5th grade and I knew something had to change. She wrote,

> Days without a daddy is sometimes hard, some days I sit and cry, don't ask me why. I feel as though he let me down, I feel like I have lost my princess crown. I want to be a daddy's girl with him buying jewelry like diamonds and pearls. When I do see him, he treats me like a queen, by that I'm saying he's never mean. His act and appeal is so unreal. Is he uncomfortable around me? I don't understand and I cannot see. I love him dearly, he's my daddy. But days are hard without a male here so, I won't let another take your place for real though. Daddy why'd you leave me, why'd you go? (Sequoya Graham).

These words pierced my heart, they broke me down, they opened up my wounded soul, and I felt like I was about to have open heart surgery. It was at that moment that I discovered the scarred tissue had the ability to affect generations if it was not dealt with early on. I laid myself on the altar for God to begin putting my fragile heart back together. This time the enemy would come greater, stronger, with more force, and I would welcome him into my heart like a familiar friend. I gave birth to my second daughter right in the recovery stage of my life. God was doing a major work in me and before the anesthesia could wear off, I was seeking the love of yet another. When would I learn to trust and never doubt? A glutton for punishment some would say, ignorant and destitute, I would declare.

Deceptive Love was where I found myself this go round. Yeah, long before Deception came to TV, I had already penned this topic in my journal. The year was 1998 and from the looks of things, I was getting my life back. This man would do whatever he could to win my affection. I knew this time would be different because I wasn't giving him the time of day. I could care less that he was fine, flawless, and had a smile that would melt any woman's heart. He could be all of that, but I wasn't interested in the least bit. It took time and he didn't mind waiting. He won me over and I was smitten…again! It was better; in fact, it was great. The first year and half was phenomenal. I thought I was well on my way to being a Mrs. to the right one this time. But the deception came full throttle and dropped right in my lap and I was crushed, devastated, and a fool once again. However, this time I was not bitter, angry or broken; I was seeking redemption.

Here I was a mother, now with two daughters who could ultimately walk around with this same condition if I didn't do something and do it quick. I already knew how to pray; I already knew who God was for myself; but, this time, I learned what to pray and how to be deliberate and intentional in my prayer life. It was a state of emergency! My daughters ran the risk of inheriting my scarred tissue and I could not stand idly by and watch that happen. I would declare war against the enemy and take back all that he had stolen from me. If they were going to grow up watching and learning from me, it would be under the guidance and leading of the Holy Spirit. I needed wisdom on how to raise my daughters healthy and vibrant. The abundant life would not be theirs if I was still scarred. I needed to be healed and whole.

The first thing I did was started the process by writing. In every situation and trial, I walked away with my head down and lived defeated. But God gave me a voice, so I started to journal all that I had been through, prayed about, and heard in sermons and teachings. Then I started reading the

Word like my life depended on it. I must have read the Book of Job so many times, I started calling myself Job. I changed my circle of influence and made sure I was connected with people who were living holy and righteous lives. I taught my daughters how to pray and prayed with them. The next thing I did was started Christian Counseling. This was the most difficult. This tried my patience and challenged me to open up. It was in the first

> ⸻⸺◦◦◦⸺⸻
>
> I HAD to *change* from the INSIDE out and the *process of purging* was NOT a pleasant one.
>
> ℀

session that I learned that I contributed a great deal to what had happened to me even though I was not the root cause. I allowed some things to happen and later perpetuated into larger crises that I had the power to stop. Don't get me wrong; counseling wasn't an immediate fix. It took four counselors for me to finally get to the one that worked well and best for me. I started and stopped, started and stopped, and started again. It was a grueling process, but God was faithful.

In the midst of all of this, I answered my call to preach and this changed my life and my speech. I had to change from the inside out and the process of purging was not a pleasant one. Each level of the journey intensified as God had to burn some things off of me. I presented my life as a living sacrifice, holy, pleasing, and acceptable unto God, my reasonable service (see Romans 12:1-2). It was not easy; it still isn't easy, but I have made peace with God and with myself. Each day I choose to forget the past and continue pressing on. The next thing that I did was to apologize to my daughters. Some would argue that this was not necessary. I say that it was and is. I submit to parents this word of advice: never be too big to apologize to your children for what YOU have caused. My daughters did not ask to be born nor did they choose their parents, but their mother was no ignorant woman; although, she was foolish. I chose their fathers, both of them. I ignored the signs and I remained in unhealthy relationships and I exposed them to nonsense. So I needed to apologize for the role I played in their upbringing that may or may not have left scars or wounds for them. I constantly remind them of who God says they are; that they are fearfully and wonderfully made in the image and likeness of God (see Psalms 139:14). They need to be reminded that nothing, absolutely nothing can separate them from the love of God which is in Christ Jesus (see Romans 8:38-39).

With each passing day, it is important for my daughters to know that their mother has scarred tissues that have caused her great pain and affliction, but she became the woman with an issue of blood and she reached out for the hem of Jesus' garment so that she could be made whole (see Matthew 9). I am far from perfect. I am so unworthy of His love, grace, mercy, and kindness, but He saved me and I'm so glad He did. I said a few pages back that I wondered why God hadn't done something in all of this and maybe He did and I didn't notice. Well, He did…He kept me in the midst of it all. He didn't let me die, He didn't let me kill anyone, and He didn't take my mind, my joy, or my peace. He didn't let my children die, He didn't let me get on a train and leave them. He kept me and in keeping me every day, He ministers to my scarred tissue and He's healing me, mending the pieces of my brokenness. He reminds me even still, that I will love again. He will send me genuine, authentic, Godly love when He sees fit. In the meantime, He loves me unconditionally

> *He* KEPT ME and IN KEEPING ME *every day*, *He* MINISTERS *to my scarred tissue.*

and I love Him without reservation. My sisters, be encouraged…God can and He will. He's doing it for me right now and He will do the same for you…I'm a witness! Today, I am draping myself in a ministry to women to share my story so that other women can find hope in my testimony. I was ordained in the African Methodist Episcopal Church in April, 2012. I was accepted to Howard University School of Divinity that same year and have just completed my first year of studies. I have become an entrepreneur and the best is still yet to come. I continue to speak life even with scarred tissue. I'm being made whole. Say it with me, Lord make me over again!

Patrice Simmons
Author: My Struggle to God's Glory

Patrice Simmons is an author, speaker, wife, mother, sister, daughter, and friend, who happens to also be very compassionate, loving, and funny. She works hard, living life with purpose and meaning, for which God has created her to do. Patrice lives in Maryland with her four children. You may reach her by email at patricesimmons72@gmail.com or patrice. simmons@rocketmail.com or by phone at 443-675-8641.

STORY 5

My Struggle to God's Glory

For many years I didn't know the calling on my life. I had to go through many challenges and trials in order for God to get me to a place of knowing who I am as an individual and what my purpose is as a whole.

Faith is the main thing to have in order to move forward and tap into your purpose. The conditions we face in life do not define us. They make us stronger and mature us to be better human beings. Our experiences we encounter are not who we are but grow us to become life learners and teachers for the kingdom. Sometimes, it shines the light on the dark places that have no growth there.

> To make the right choices in life, you have to get in touch with your soul. To do this, you need to experience solitude, which most people are afraid of, because in the silence you hear the truth and know the solutions.
>
> Deepak Chopra

Life is too ironic. It takes sadness to know what happiness is, noise to appreciate silence, and absence to value presence.

I remember getting myself geared up to write my part in this book, and that week, I was dealing with so many things that I had never encountered before. My little cousin's mother passed away. She had been in a coma for several years due to getting hit by a car when her daughter was six, who is now 14. It left her daughter heart-broken. Then my father had been ill and in the hospital for over a week, due to having gout so bad, that it left him crippled and unable to walk. It was scarier for me to deal with the possibility of my dad dying from this. But God turned things around on my dad's behalf and gave him a second chance at life.

My youngest son's father lost his job and was facing the possibility of being homeless and on the streets. He hadn't seen our son in months due to me living three hours from him. Stressed out from life and not knowing God as his source of refugee, he almost committed suicide. He left a note on his mom's car explaining that he felt worthless and unwanted by anyone, and this world would be better without him.

He was found on a highway in the middle of the night by a police officer with two cuts on him, but he was alive. At that moment, I felt if he was found dead, my son would grow up without a father; not knowing where he came from and what a relationship between father and son is like. But God saved him and turned things around for his good. It's interesting because anything you do for God comes with a price and you will suffer for the kingdom.

The enemy had things going bad for me at my job. My boss changed my schedule on me right around the time I was to focus on this project, of course, to distract me. I was going to lose hours and money because I wasn't going to be getting anymore overtime from this change. They would sometimes even ask me if I wanted to leave early even if I hadn't worked eight hours yet. I was only getting 28 hours and now they wanted to turn it into less than that. The type of work I do is a Pharmacy Rx clerk, filling prescriptions and dealing with medicine. I've been at my job for ten years, and I've had my schedule changed at least three times. It never really bothered me before like it did this time, or should I say, it allowed the enemy to control my mind and the way I thought about it.

Every shift I've had has been over night. It allows me to get my children from school and take them to doctors' appointments. Like I mentioned before, this time was very different for me. I was angry about the change and thought about how much difference in pay I would get. I took it into prayer knowing that God was in control. I was being tested by God just on how much faith I had in Him to supply my needs, knowing that in His timing, everything would work out. Even still, I was tried by the enemy by his attacks to keep me at a place of no hope or no way of overcoming life's difficulties and challenges. He didn't stop!

Our marriage and children, along with my finances, all came under attack. My oldest son, who had never really given me much trouble, was starting to give me a lot of attitude whenever I would ask him to do something or walk around the house in a bad mood, along with being disrespectful. I know how preteens can be, especially at this stage of them becoming more into their own. But to me, it seemed like a shift had taken place in my son that wasn't present before. Then my marriage was being attacked financially like never before. My hours being cut and me not bringing home what I used to, made it harder because my husband and I were separated at the time, but his checks were being garnished due to not passing eviction and owing the company money. Rent wasn't being paid on that month and the court filing for the rent was against us. My landlord, who once was very understanding to me, became my worst enemy.

He came to my home asking for the rent money when he knew we didn't have it, telling me if I didn't have the money in twenty days, he was going to put us out. He said things like, "You people; I don't get you. We're already giving you a deal with the rent and you can't pay that." It's not about not having the money or paying the rent, it's the principle, how he handled us, and his approach. Did I mention that we didn't have any heat in the house and didn't have hot water as well for four months during the winter season, with four children in the house? This wasn't okay. My water heater had gone bad and we did not know the heater was on the verge of this happening before we moved in. Imagine being in a house with young children in the winter. My youngest one was one-month-old. So I had to heat his milk on our heater, had to boil our children's water, then put it in a gallon jug so they could take a bath. We discussed this with our landlord, asking to fix the problem, and when they finally did, after those cold, four months, our thermostat stopped working.

He told me to turn the oven on. I'm not going to do anything until we get rent money. I've been there for three years, never once had a problem with paying the rent, and they knew our situation but didn't seem to care. God told me to pray, "No weapon formed against me will prosper." His will was done on my behalf. I remained in the home. The court dismissed the case and I didn't have to pay that month's rent that the Landlord was asking for because

NEVER LOSE *faith;*
Believe in the
IMPOSSIBLE.

he never showed up. We still live there and our finances have increased. My husband is back working, my son's attitude improved, and his behavior returned to himself. God is forever faithful to his Word. All it requires us to do is never lose faith; believe in the impossible. There is always a light at the end of every dark tunnel in our lives. I and my sister have seemed to have a rocky road relationship. There were times I wondered if she had real love for me because the pain I had encountered with her, I didn't fully understand. A time came when my sister asked me to co-sign a car for her. I was about 19-years-old, my credit was in great condition, and I agreed to sign this car for her. Well about six months later, the car company called me and asked for the payments on the car to be made very soon or they were going to take the vehicle.

I was puzzled and confused as to what they were telling me because my sister was working a full-time job. We worked at the same company and she assured me that the payments were going to be made on time. As I began to explain to the lady that I had no knowledge of this because I was just the co-signer on this car and didn't have anything to do with this situation, she went through the history of my sister's record. She told me there were only three months' worth of payments made on the car and they had been sending letters to her and calling her about the issue. She was speaking with me about helping with the payments. I guess I had a lot to do with this than I thought. I couldn't believe what I was hearing. Not only didn't my sister mention to me about the issue at hand, she told me everything was okay and the payments were being made on time. Talk about betrayal and lying. How could she do this to me? I didn't own a car and now my credit was in jeopardy. When I finally got around to asking my sister about this, she told me, "I've been having financial problems and can't afford to pay for this car anymore." I said to her, "Why didn't you tell me this from the beginning? I see you at work every day. We could have figured something out." Now I can't help because they are asking for over 3,000 dollars in back payments. With no real solution from my sister, they took the car; however, they gave us 30 days to claim it back. I called the place up where the car was at. I had just recently received my income tax money and decided to take that money and pay to get the car back. After all, she had my nephew who was one-year-old at the time, and I didn't want to see her struggle to find rides to get him and herself to work.

Even though I was in the same situation, I didn't have a car, and my son was two-years-old. But God, and my love for my sister, told me to do the right thing. So the company took the money and released the car back to her. She thanked me for helping her and said that she wouldn't miss anymore payments and would come to me if trouble arose again. I said okay and for about four months the payments were being made on time.

When God is for you the enemy will be against you. One day, I receive a letter in the mail explaining the car was getting ready to be repossessed due to non-payments. The amount this time was around $2,000 dollars for three months of non-payment. My sister had received a raise at work so I thought this couldn't be true. It was and they took the car and came after me and my sister for the remaining balance of $15,000 dollars. I didn't have the money so they put it on my credit. So my credit score went from 700 to 400. This car damaged the credit I had worked so hard to get it where it once was. To have somebody who didn't do right by what they had really hurt me. I was angry with my sister. I did all I could do to help out and all she told me was they took her car and said they put it on my credit too. She didn't take reasonability for what she had done knowing if I didn't help her with co-signing the car, she wouldn't have had it. I wanted to buy a house and that dream just seemed to fade away. I had to file for bankruptcy, which stayed on my credit for ten years. I wasn't able to get anything. I held a lot of unforgiveness in my heart towards my sister because I was there for her. How could she do this to me? I never really got the apology I felt I deserved but as I grew closer to God, He spoke to me one day. "You have two choices: either forgive your sister with all your heart or stay in this pain and never grow into a better place in me." I argued with God about this for some time because I wanted God to understand how I

Forgive with all your heart or STAY *in this pain* and NEVER *grow* into *a better place* in *Me*.

was feeling. How many times have you held a person in unforgiveness in such a way that we debate with God about doing the right thing? It's very vital that we obey Him so He can get the glory out of it! He already knew how I was feeling and needed me to release the pain.

God continues to do a good work in me. I sincerely forgave her, decided not to relive the pain, and chose to have a better relationship with my sister. At the end of the day, God paid a heavy price so we can enjoy our lives and be free doing it. Don't let the cares of this world keep you in bondage or bound in any way! The enemy wants to kill, steal, and destroy your future. God is our healer and he can renew any wounded "heart". Trust in him!

I remember a time when I had a close to death experience. Honestly, I've had many attacks on my life: growing up being verbally abused by my mom, seeing her physically abuse my step-father, along with my oldest son's father trying to kill me when I was 19 with a kitchen knife. But this close to death experience I'm referring to was more physical. I was driving home from work just like I would do any other day. But this day was certainly different. As I approached the traffic light, it went from green to red instantly, and the way my car was, I couldn't move out of harm's way so I was stuck with oncoming traffic. Cars were coming from different directions and here I am in the middle of the busy intersection facing death! Yes and my mind was all over the place. I was praying to God to keep me. At one point, I closed my eyes because if this was going to be the end for me, I didn't want to see it. How many of you could have weathered this alone? Without God's help, I wouldn't be here talking about this. And as we all know prayer changes things. In an instant, God saved me. A police officer came to my rescue, but I know God sent him to me.

When I opened my eyes, I saw the officer blocking the intersection off for me. He proceeded to ask me what happened. I explained to him that I was traveling with the other cars and as I'm about to drive across the intersection, the light turned red. I couldn't move my car because I was too far out. He responded by saying, "You are lucky to still be alive." I had to let him know it wasn't luck, but the lord saving and keeping me. I thanked him for coming to my rescue. What I learned from all of this is to remember that God always has your back and certainly, whenever there is a calling on your life, the enemy is going to do whatever he can to destroy that. I have to say my belief and love for God and how much he will cease any attack from the enemy, took me to another level with Him. I just thank Him for how much precious life is and I will never take anything for granted.

Many difficult situations in my life have brought about negative outcomes and not using wisdom has taken me to things that I shouldn't have involved myself in. Having all the warning signs present but not heeding any of them caused me to marry a person who God didn't ordain as my husband. Instead, I chose him because I wanted things in my own timing and not His timing. As a result, the marriage became a tragedy. I have been married for six years and separated for a year and a half. In the beginning of my marriage, it was very dark and lonely. The enemy had attacked our marriage on many levels. There was a lot of verbal abuse and our finances struggled. My husband was a drunk and a smoker. We didn't get married to God's glory nor did we have Christ in the center of our marriage. Our children at the time were very young. My daughter was two-years-old when we got married. She and my son, who was six years old at the time, saw a lot of things that no child should have to ever witness or deal with.

Our home was a very unpleasant place to be. On a daily basis, my husband would disrespect me in front of my kids which really made the kids sad. Often times, they would ask me why I was crying. It hurt me even more to know their young tender hearts were starting to be broken from what they were seeing. He also belittled me and even at times threatened to hit me. I really would see the enemy coming out when that happened. Any type of verbal, abusive way he could hurt me, he would, because of his unhappiness and the feelings of failure he experienced in his life; he took those feelings out on me.

He drank mainly to ease the pain from reality and passed out from it every day. It got to a point where I stopped being mad about his passing out drunk every day and just acted like the problem wasn't there. I and my husband lived as roommates for many years, not as a married couple should. The love was distances away and our kids weren't seeing us as pleasant with each other in a way that God would want things to be in a home. It was time for me to make a serious change. I couldn't go on like this; I was starting to get suicidal thoughts and I felt as if my life wasn't going to get any better. I thought all the issues in my marriage and how my husband treated me were a result of my being the problem. And what was going on with us was too big for God to change. My mind-set was wrong, and I couldn't get away from it. I even thought about killing him and how I was going to do it…especially when he would make me mad. He knew how to push my buttons, but I couldn't bring myself to do that. I needed to leave our home so I could clear my mind and allow God to change me.

I stayed at a shelter for about three months. My first time being there wasn't a bad thing as I thought it would be. The place wasn't clean, but I had a peace of mind that I didn't have for a long time. At that time, I shared rooms with eight other women; one of them had a young baby around five-months-old. I never experienced anything like this before for it was a totally new environment for me. I encountered women who were on drugs, abused victims, and some with many children with no dads around. I discussed with these women the things I had been going through, my marriage, and why I couldn't stay at my home. They also shared why they were there. I truly love how God will use you to be a blessing to somebody else even in the midst of your own pain.

That is what He was doing to me. I found that my struggles and suicidal thoughts were nothing compared to what these women had faced. For example, we had a group meeting one night and this lady explained to everyone that being at the shelter wasn't a place she could ever have imagined herself being in, especially with having her granddaughter there with her.

The little girl couldn't have been any more than seven. So she goes on to say that her daughter was murdered by the hands on her granddaughter's father. Her daughter was physically abused by him often and she would have to take her to the hospital because he would beat her real bad. But this time, he snapped.

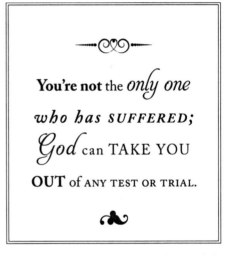

You're not the *only one who has* SUFFERED; *God* can TAKE YOU **OUT** of ANY TEST OR TRIAL.

They had to go in hiding from him because he wanted to kill the little girl who saw what had happened to her mom and as she is telling us this, my heart dropped. I couldn't believe that such evil exists in the world. But the real revelation I received was: you're not the only one who has suffered, and God can take you out of any mess, test, or trial. The suicidal thoughts, feeling lost in my marriage, unloved, not needed, and the verbal abuse had me dying inside. Growing up being physically abused, from the hands of my mother, was really more towards my step-father than towards me. But I witnessed it all. My child's father and now my husband, who verbally abused me, is nothing! I mean nothing could ever compare to the loss this lady felt from losing her child! My times at the shelter showed me the reality of this world and what is important in life: family. I needed to go and see that I wasn't the only one suffering and to release what God placed inside of me to bless the women there. Healing is truly a process. I did divorce my husband because I discovered the value of loving one's self and knew God had a better plan for my life!

It could become such a tragedy when we allow ourselves to be deceived or misguided by the wrong people who we think has our backs. There was a time I had to stay with a relative due to losing my place. And this

God DOESN'T want *us to* R U N *when things start* to become PAINFUL.

was not something I didn't think nor would have thought to be any kind of trouble to me because we were family. I'm not the type of person who asks for things or go to people when in need. Maybe it's a pride thing, not really sure, but I always like to do things for myself and don't usually wait around for others to help. This time I couldn't avoid the help. I had no place to go with my children. When I moved in with my aunt, I explained that I only needed to stay for about two months to save enough money to move in my new place. The first week or so was good, no problems and got along well. She played with my kids and had a lot of fun together. My aunt was very spiritual; she had posters, cards, notes, music, all through her house that displayed God in some type of way. I being a very spiritual person, connected with her and we talked about the goodness of the Lord often. Whatever is in the heart of a man will always come out at some point. That's when things changed for the worst for me. She told me that her contract had breached due to me living there and not being on the lease. I had to be out in two weeks. She was lying. I was no longer welcomed there by her. Only her! I never met anyone from the leasing office and no paperwork saying I had to leave. I had not done anything to her. I cooked and cleaned the house. I felt hurt, totally lost, and I was no longer comfortable there. I wanted to leave immediately, but had nowhere to go. Each day felt more painful and hard to deal with. She stopped talking to me and the kids. I had to ask God to give me the strength to do this. I realized she had a lot of hurt feelings going on inside of her and I just got in the way of her mess. God needed me to see her for what she was and where prayer was going to be needed at. She carried strongholds, depression, and two of her kids were locked up at the time.

And she took that out on me. I had to forgive her, and when I finally left her house, I thanked her for allowing me to stay there.

Sometimes in life, God doesn't want us to run when things start to become painful. We have to go through so that he can evaluate us to make His name great in the midst of the battle! I encourage you all that are reading my story to see that no matter what the enemy tried to bring my way or what adversities I faced, I didn't give up. I stayed strong in every situation that life threw my way. And you can too! Life isn't fair at times but don't let it get the best of you! Never allow yourself to get stuck in your storms.

Don't give the enemy any of that negative energy because it's only a test from God. Trust in his timing, rely on his promises, wait for his answers, believe in his miracles, rejoice in his goodness, and relax in his presence. The most important thing to do when problem arises is to pray until you see the break through. No matter how many trials and tribulations that come your way, always seek God! "Now faith is the assurance of things hoped for, the conviction of things not seen" (Hebrews 11:1, NKJV). It doesn't matter how long it takes. Trust in God's timing.

TURN
your w o u n d s
into WISDOM

"And Jesus said to them, 'Because of the littleness of your faith; for truly I say to you, if you have faith as a mustard seed, you shall say to this mountain, move from here to there, and it shall move; and nothing shall be impossible to you'" (Matthew 17:20, NKJV). Speak life over yourself. Stay humble through life's dark seasons.

From every wound there is a scar, and every scar tells a story. It is a story that says, "I have survived". The greatest achievement for any human being is to love God and each other.

Turn your wounds into wisdom. And above all else, always believe in yourself because you, too, can "Walk in your Purpose".

Dr. Terri Collins
Author: Leaving My Fears Behind Me

Dr. Terri Collins is an accomplished Licensed Professional Counselor in Georgia. She works in corrections providing therapy for inmates diagnosed with mental illnesses. Dr. Collins is also an adjunct professor for Grand Canyon University's Professional Counseling program and a therapist/consultant for Alcovy Spring Counseling Services, where she provides family and individual therapy. She can be reached by telephone at (678) 938-8809 or by email at terric47@msn.com.

STORY 6

LEAVING My **Fears** Behind Me

Have you ever been so passionate in wanting something that you discovered you had to face and overcome many obstacles just to get what you wanted? Or have you ever experienced a time in your life where your sole desire to reach your goal obliterated your self-doubts and fears about attaining that goal? I experienced this when I made the decision to become Dr. Terri Collins.

The highest academic degree an individual can obtain is the Doctor of Philosophy degree or Ph.D. The decision to work on a doctorate should not be taken lightly. When one decides to pursue a Ph.D., he or she will face a demanding commitment to complete required course work and write an extensive dissertation. A dissertation is not a mere college "report"; it is a lengthy research document that outlines the findings of one's study. A student is required to get approval from his or her dissertation committee throughout the entire writing of the dissertation. Working on a dissertation could possibly take up to seven to 10 years. One must devote an enormous amount of time and dedication while working on her doctorate. Many people who begin in a doctoral program do not finish because of the emotional demands, time commitment, and monetary requirements.

I decided to get my doctorate for many reasons. First, I wanted the academic challenge. I had just completed my Master of Arts program in Counseling and wanted to continue my education. I also dreamed of having my own private practice where I would provide therapy for emotionally distressed individuals, and I wanted to be considered an expert in my field. I felt having a doctorate would enhance my professional standing. I also knew a doctorate would enable me to use my skills to uplift God's Kingdom. I realized the process would be a challenge, it would take several years to complete, and the cost of going back to school would be expensive. But, I believed I could earn my doctorate with hard work and with God by my side. It took me ten long and challenging years to complete my doctoral program. I learned several aspects about myself during the years I worked on my degree, and I am thankful for the life lessons that followed.

> *I encountered* and OVERCAME ALL *of my fears* with the *Lord* *by my side.*

While working on my dissertation, I had to face and overcome many of my fears. For example, I feared the death of my parents, I feared being financially unstable, and I feared having health problems. I also realized that my biggest weakness was to refuse to face my fear of believing and thinking that I was not good enough. I encountered and overcame all of these fears with the Lord by my side. Although I faced these fears while working on my doctorate, I discovered that none of them would be as crippling to my personal, professional, and spiritual growth, as my fear of being "found out" by others that I was not worthy. Although I was loved and supported by my family, and I achieved many of my goals, I always had a vague thought I was "just not good enough." This self-defeating thought would hover in my mind while I worked, corresponded with my colleagues, and socialized with my friends.

This fear eventually became my secret – one that I did not want anyone to discover. I took exceptional measures to guard this secret from other people. I avoided speaking about topics, events, and situations that I had knowledge of because I feared my secret would be revealed. In work situations, I shied away from offering my opinion on subjects so that others could not see through me, notice my flaws and reject me, or tell others about my secret. As a result, I stayed quiet and on many occasions did not seek help from others even if I needed it because I did not want them to uncover my secret. It wasn't until I started working on my dissertation that I learned I was doing more harm by harboring these negative thoughts and preventing myself from taking more productive courses of action.

I did not realize that I suffered from this fear until I began working on my dissertation. Going back to school to get my doctorate was not an easy decision for me. I had just completed my master's in counseling program, and I was in the midst of changing my career from banking to counseling in corrections. I was transitioning from working with bankers to working with bank robbers. This change was exciting for me because I truly believed that counseling was my calling. I knew that the Lord wanted me to be a counselor, and I witnessed Him open doors for me to get my first counseling position at an adult detention center. Soon after starting that job, my practicum supervisor asked me to work with her in her private counseling practice, which was both a surprise and a dream come true for me. I always wanted to be in private practice, and now I had a great opportunity to do just that. What more could I ask for? I was starting my new career, in a job that I loved going to every day, and I also had an opportunity to begin building clientele for my own private practice.

While working at the detention center, two of my colleagues told me about an online doctoral program with Walden University. They encouraged me to continue my education and get my doctorate. In 1999, online programs were relatively new; therefore, I was leery about the legitimacy of the school's Health Psychology program. Many people at that time did not look at the online doctorate programs as being "real"

Ph.D. programs. I was not sure if I would be taken seriously or viewed as competent in my field of study if I attended an online school. It was scary to think that people may see me as incompetent in my field, the field that I knew that God called me to do. Although I did not know in what capacity God wanted me to use my doctorate degree, I knew I was obtaining it to help uplift God's Kingdom. I wanted to get my Ph.D., but I also knew that I needed to work to pay my bills. Therefore I decided to enroll in the online Health Psychology Ph.D. program at Walden University, which would allow me to continue working at the detention center.

I was determined to be knowledgeable in my field; therefore, no one would be able to question my opinion or, worst of all, see my flaws and discover my secret. When one of my interns found out that I decided to return to school, she shared with me the scripture of Jeremiah 29:11; "For I know the plans for you," declares the Lord, "plans to prosper you and not to harm you." Then I truly knew that getting my doctorate was part of God's plan to work in His Kingdom. Just as He opened doors for me in my career, He would continue to bless me and see me complete my doctorate.

In the beginning of my doctorate program, the sessions were overwhelming and I began to wonder if I had the drive, the determination, and more importantly, the confidence to go through the program. When I began to question my decision to get my doctorate, I would remember the scripture of Jeremiah 29:11 and knew that getting my doctorate was not about me but about doing God's work.

I would often go through periods where I had reservations, little thoughts telling me, "Girl, you don't belong in this program." As a result, I often would not tell people I was in a doctorate program because I feared many people in my field would not take me seriously. At times my insecurities were so great, I would cry to my mother that I did not know what I was getting into and that enrolling in the doctoral program had been a huge mistake. My mother always reassured me and reminded me that God would not get me to this point and then leave me. Just hearing the comforting words from my mother gave me confidence I could complete this program.

I encountered many obstacles while working on my dissertation. Many of them delayed my progress and offset my graduation date. As I confronted these obstacles, I always remembered the scripture of Jeremiah 29:11 and I would tell myself that quitting was not an option because getting my doctorate was part of a bigger plan, not simply a personal goal.

When I began writing my dissertation, my first committee chairman was fired by the university. I didn't think this was a serious setback because I was just beginning on my dissertation. The university assigned another chairman for my committee, and I agreed to this decision because I wanted to move forward on my dissertation. However, after working with the new chairman for a couple of months, I realized that I was not progressing with my dissertation as I expected. After praying about the situation, I decided to replace my committee chairman. This decision turned out to be a blessing because my newest chairman brought on another member to my dissertation committee who was an expert on my dissertation topic and who agreed to allow me to use his agency's archived data for my research. During all of this transition, I knew that God was guiding me and would not abandon me. I was excited that I had God's favor in getting my dissertation committee in place.

I was doing well with writing my dissertation, but unfortunately by the time I completed the second chapter, I began to doubt my abilities. The paralyzing fear of not being competent to complete my dissertation began to eat away at me. I had to push back my negative thoughts, fight my feelings of inadequacy, and remember that God had given me all that I needed to complete my dissertation.

By the time I got to the third chapter of my dissertation, this ugly fear again showed its face to me. The third chapter covered the statistics aspect of my research. My fear dragged me down, and eventually I stopped working on the chapter. I went through periods where I would make myself work on my dissertation, but I was not making any significant progress.

I reached a point where I was doing minimal work on my dissertation. I was no longer looking at my scripture for motivation. Then a devastating blow I never imagined I would go through came: the death of my mother. I feared not having her support, not being able to hear her comforting words. For awhile, I wondered how I would be able to go on without her love and encouragement. She loved me unconditionally and now I did not have her in my life. During this time in my life, I was so grief stricken; I was just going through the motions. I was unable to think about my dissertation, and I suffered deep regrets about my mother not seeing me become Dr. Collins. In addition, I began to worry about the wellbeing of my father since he lost his wife of 47 years. Eventually I got strength from God to continue on in my life. I constantly prayed to God for strength and I found comfort in knowing that my mother knew the Lord. I was reminded once again God would not leave me alone, and He would not put me through anything that I could not bear.

After the death of my mother, another obstacle in the form of financial problems emerged. I was frequently away from my home in Georgia for extended periods of time to check on my father. I was also living with my sister at that time. When bad times befell her and she lost her job, most of the finances for the upkeep of our home fell on me. All of this occurred during a time when I was changing jobs and did not receive a paycheck for a little over a month. My savings were depleted by this time because I was commuting back and forth from Georgia to Maryland to check on my father.

Soon my sister and I were two months behind on our mortgage. I stayed out of school for a couple of quarters due to this situation. I began working a part-time job in addition to my full-time job to try to get back on track. Working an additional job squeezed the time available for me to work on my dissertation. When I explained the situation to my dissertation chairman, he responded that he understood and to let him know when I would be able to enroll back into school.

During this time that I was worrying constantly about keeping our home, I did not work on my dissertation. Once again I allowed my fears of what others would say about me get the best of me. I did not reach out to any of my friends because I did not want any of them to see me as irresponsible or incompetent in managing my finances. My sister and I requested financial relief from our mortgage company, but were not given any help. Eventually, we were facing possible foreclosure of our home, which only caused additional emotional distress. I could not sleep at night because I worried about losing our house, and I worried what people would say if they knew about my situation. Due to my insecurity, I kept this secret to myself as well.

After worrying about our mortgage situation for a couple of months, I realized I was not trusting in God to see me through this situation. I began to pray and believe God would provide a solution for us. One day the mortgage company called about our late payments. When I explained our situation to the collector, he immediately began the process for us to receive assistance from the mortgage company. I could not rest until we were officially told that an agreement was accepted and that our house would not go into foreclosure. However, after this situation, I learned that worrying was unproductive and I needed to give my problems to God.

I tried to get back into the routine of working on my dissertation. Although I was not officially enrolled in class at that time, I made a personal goal to work on my dissertation so that I would have the first three chapters completed by the time I returned to school.

Yet another challenge loomed for me though, when I encountered physical illness. I was determined to start the New Year right and decided to celebrate my 40th birthday. The day of my birthday, I began to experience chest pains. I told myself that the chest pains were just anxiety. However, a few weeks after my birthday celebration, I experienced several more episodes of chest pains whenever I worked out. When I finally went to the doctor, extensive testing revealed that I had a clogged artery and I was immediately scheduled for angioplasty surgery. I did not withdraw from school at this time. Although the doctors told me that I could do light work immediately after my surgery, I avoided working on my dissertation stating that I needed time to recover from my surgery.

For a year, I worked intermittently on my dissertation. I feared completing the third chapter of my dissertation because that meant that I would have to do my first defense for my research. The thought of doing my defense terrified me because I did not want my committee to think that I did not understand my subject matter.

By the spring quarter of 2007, tuition for classes had soared, and once again I was unable to pay for my course. I notified my dissertation chairman I would not be able to register due to financial hardship. We agreed I would continue to work on my dissertation and by the time I enrolled in class again, we would be ready for the dissertation committee to review my first three chapters.

A couple of months later, I attempted to contact my chairman to let him know about my progress (or, more accurately, lack of progress). When he finally responded to me, he stated that he could no longer work with me because my dissertation was progressing too slowly. He had never given me a warning about his concerns. I tried pleading with him but he refused to continue in the role as chairman. So there I was left without a chairman. I contacted the other committee member and asked him if he could take over as my chairman. He also told me that he could not remain on my committee. At the same time, he discouraged me from pursuing getting the data from his agency because it was now almost impossible for non-Federal employees to conduct research with the agency. I was seemingly left with no options or avenues of getting similar data that I needed, thus essentially killing my dissertation.

This latest blow was devastating for me. I had no chairman, I was down a committee member, and I had no source of data for my research. I spent seven years in this program and now my dissertation was dead. At first I did not tell anyone what I was going through because I feared what they would think about me. I did not know what to do, but I began to pray and expect a miracle. I talked to God and told Him how I really felt, that I was scared.

After going to God, I began to find peace. I was no longer angry with my chairman because I now saw this as an opportunity for all to see God's glory. I realized that the situation must be part of God's plan and that something better would come out of it. Quitting at this point was not an option, because getting my dissertation was not just for me, but it was for my work in God's Kingdom. I slowly began to conquer my fear of what others would say about my situation because I now began to realize that I needed help. I talked to my aunt and told her my fears, and the top one on my list was that people see me as a joke or laugh at me because of the money and years that I spent on this dissertation. She assured me that I was loved by the ones that mattered and that if people talked, it would not kill me. These simple words made all of the sense in the world.

In conquering my fear, I then contacted a friend who had recently completed his doctorate in the same program. He was able to suggest a company for me to contact for archived data to use for my research. This was almost too good to be true. I realized if I allowed my fear to control me, as I had been doing for years, I would not have received this important information. I also realized that there are individuals who are genuine and willing to help me achieve my goals. They are not out to deride or undercut me – perhaps they are part of a bigger plan as well.

I could not afford to have any more setbacks. Once I contacted the company about using their data, they immediately offered to help me. The next two years I worked hard on rewriting my dissertation. Each time I began to doubt my abilities, I referred to my scripture of Jeremiah 29:11 and I remembered that God placed everything in perfect order for me to complete my dissertation. By the time it came for me to do my first defense, I was preparing for another surgery. I wanted to defend before this surgery, but was unable to do so. I did not get discouraged; instead I used my time off from work to prepare for my defense. My first defense turned out to be easy for me. I realized I needed to continue to conquer my fears by facing them, by simply pushing myself to move on.

> *I realized*
> *I needed to continue*
> to CONQUER MY FEARS
> by FACING THEM,
> *by simply*
> PUSHING MYSELF
> to MOVE ON!

I continued to struggle with getting financing to complete my dissertation. Several quarters I had to sit out from school because I could not pay for the course, but I did not get discouraged because I knew that God would not bring me to this point and then abandon me.

Fear loomed once again as I started work on the last two chapters of my dissertation. I was not strong in math, and I knew that I had to analyze the statistics for my data. Several nights I came to tears while trying to interpret data or to relate the outcome of the data to society. Soon, I realized that

I was reverting to my old, bad behavior of not seeking help from others. I went outside my comfort zone and asked for help once again. In no time, I found a graduate student who was willing to help me interpret my data results. For months, I worked my day job, came home, slept for an hour, and then got back up to work on my dissertation. Many times I would cry. Many times I would procrastinate, but I would immediately remind myself that God chose me to do work in His Kingdom, and most importantly, I am worthy in doing this for Him.

On May 25, 2010, my dissertation was conferred. After my defense, my committee stated that I had the "smoothest" defense. I answered all of their questions with such ease and confidence because I now knew that I was competent and that I was supported by God. I started my dissertation as the woman who did not have anything to say because of the fear of others thinking I was a fake or incompetent. I was the woman who feared that people would find out my secret and believed that hiding within me would be the answer. Working on my dissertation taught me that I would encounter many trials and obstacles in life. Some obstacles or events may seem so devastating that I would fear I would not have the strength in me to go on. But I learned that I get my strength from Jesus. I learned that although I knew that Jesus was by my side, I did not fully trust that He was there with me. I began to see that God was always by my side and that He never left me alone to struggle. My fears were irrational and without basis. God paved the way for me to complete my dissertation so that I could do more work in His Kingdom. With Him by my side, I do not have to worry what other people think about me. Very importantly, I also learned that not everyone will be against me. I would have missed critical opportunities if I had stayed to myself and not asked for help, especially during this process. For me, finding assistance from others only provided more praises to God. I was complete then and now. I just needed to know it for myself by truly and firmly putting my trust in God in my life. I recommend for women who suffer with self-defeating thoughts and insecurities to put their trust in God. Whenever there are moments of doubts, tell God about your fears. He will not reject you; He will love you, comfort you, and be with you throughout all of your obstacles. I also recommend, for any woman who decides to work toward a doctorate, that she prepares herself to embrace the long journey of endless hours of research, financial commitment, and even emotional distress. She should always remember that "life will happen," but God will be your strength and will be by your side, leading you to your goal.

Sharon E. Willingham
Author: Silent No More

Sharon E. Willingham is a woman who is passionate about teaching the Word of God. She ministers healing to women of domestic violence, addiction, sexual abuse, and other types of pain. Sharon is currently writing her first book that will give more in-depth information of her life story. This is her first published work. For speaking engagements, she can be reached at sharon.willingham@yahoo.com.

STORY 7

SILENT
No More

"We know that all things (good and bad) work together for the good to them that love the Lord and who are called according to his purpose!" (Romans 8:28, emphasis mine).

On average, more than three women a day are murdered by the hands of their husbands or boyfriends in the United States. In 2005, 1,181 women were murdered.

Nearly one in four women in the United States has reported experiencing violence by a current or former spouse or boyfriend at some point in their lives. I was one of those women. I have survived to tell my story and break the silence. I have hidden my suffering of abuse for many years until now (Center for Disease Control & Prevention, 2008).

We dated for two years before getting married. We met each other through a mutual friend. He was a handsome, intelligent, small business owner. We were in love with each other. We were inseparable. He decided to join the army for a possible future career.

I stayed behind to continue working and to take care of my niece, Charon. We talked to each on the phone just about every night. Our relationship was solid. We planned to get married after he finished training and was assigned to a permanent duty station in North Carolina. I moved there to be with him and I was so thrilled about us finally being together. As I arrived to North Carolina though, the lies began to start. He told me that he had an apartment for us, but to my surprise, it was a lie. He was staying at a friend's house; I was very upset. He smoothed things over with his charm and said, "I will make it up to you."

We got married on March 17, 1987. Everything was going great. He was loving, devoted, extremely smart, and focused on succeeding in his career in the Army. He was my friend, my confidant, my protector. He treated me like a queen. My husband was kind and generous to friends, family, and strangers. I never suspected that Victor had that violent rage in him. It did not show until the day he tried to choke me to death.

The abuse began a few months after we got married. We were talking in the parking lot of my job at Sears during my lunch break. I questioned him about what I found out about his possible cheating. He denied it and became very angry. Out of nowhere, he grabbed me by my neck and began to choke me. Someone witnessed what was happening and called the Army police. The officer showed up and asked me, "Ma'am, do you want to file a complaint and press charges against him. I was still in shock! Victor said to me, "If you do, I would get thrown out of the Army." I felt that it was my fault and that he would lose his job. I felt sorry for him. I didn't file a complaint. He also refused to help me with transportation as means of control. I did not tell anyone about what he had done to me. He apologized eventually and said, "I did not mean to hurt you. I will never put my hands on you again." I want you to know that was the day that I gave him control over me. That day forward, the abusive cycle began. Later, I found out he lied about the cheating; it was true.

I felt that perhaps I could change some of his behavior by showing him love and spending time with him to show him that I wanted to make our marriage works. By the time my sister, Tonya, came down to live with us in North Carolina, to spend her last year of high school there and graduate, he had begun to verbally abuse me with intensity. He messed with my mind and my emotions. I decided I was going to leave him to go back to New Jersey with my family, but found out that I was pregnant. I was extremely happy, but he was not there for me. My sister revealed to me he was having an affair. I was so furious, I went into a rage. I found out where his mistress lived and went to her house. His car was there and he would not come out. He denied everything and made up stories. I continued to stay with him even after he denied the affair. Once I had my son, I thought our relationship would grow closer, but he still continued to be unstable.

He decided that he no longer wanted to stay in the Army, so we eventually moved back to New Jersey. While moving back New Jersey, he had no stable employment, so we lost everything. The car was repossessed, the house was in foreclosure, and to add to this devastation, I was pregnant with our second child. He finally found a job. While he was working, he was having an affair and doing drugs with a woman he was working with. I found out and confronted Victor about the affair. Of course, he denied it. He became so angry and tried to strangle me while I was on the sofa. I fought and begged for my life that day. I was able to get away and he was arrested for assault. I went into depression. I did not want to live, but God spoke to me. He said, "I will never leave you nor forsake you." God said that He loved me and that my children were a blessing from Him; they need me. After God spoke to me, I left the house and moved to another state. Over periods of time, we eventually got back together. He made me a promise again to stop cheating and using drugs.

That promise was broken. He started using drugs at a terrifying rate. Only now, the hallucinations had begun. He sometimes sat all night watching out the window thinking he saw "snipers in the trees waiting to attack the house". He also began a pattern of unstable employment. The cycle began again. The severity of rage increased with time, as did his drug abuse. I had come to believe that the drugs were not the cause of his violence. He was always prone to having a violent and controlling nature. The drugs did make the mood swings more sudden and more severe. I got through that period of my life through the grace of God. Out of nowhere one day, he came home and said, "I just re-dedicated my life back to Christ."

I, too, re-dedicated my life back to the Lord in 1994. We both felt the Lord was calling us back to live in New Jersey, so we moved once again.

After years that we were married, Victor became jealous. It became increasingly apparent that he wanted my attention at all times. I was at his beck in call. I cooked, cleaned, and served him. My husband seemed to have more pent up anger as the years went on. I started to feel like I was always walking a balance beam around him. When I would try to discuss anything about how I felt, he would get agitated and turn it into an argument. I soon realized it was easier to just appease him to keep peace. I noticed the kids' demeanor changed as well as my own when my husband arrived home because we never knew what type of mood he would be in. Sometimes, he would snap for no reason.

Many times, when the violence began, my husband would seem remorseful for physically, emotionally, and verbal abusing me. He would buy me things as a sign of apology. However, as the abuse became more frequent and more torture-like in nature, he seemed to enjoy the pain and suffering he inflicted on me. I felt so alone and isolated but knew I couldn't leave or tell anyone.

From the outside looking in, we had it all. What was missing was my sense of personal safety for me. This time in our lives, God had blessed me with a hair salon that was very successful. Financially, we were doing well. As years went on, the situation grew worse. He started using drugs again. At this point, the drug use escalated and He was unstable with employment again. His episodes of extreme rage towards me became increasingly frequent. He was often lazy and selfish when it came to doing chores and helping around the house. He began entertaining young women claiming he was their counselor because they didn't have a father. He used this as an excuse to justify the affairs which I later found out about.

I told him on many occasions that it was inappropriate, but he became angrier when I questioned his judgment. Victor had the audacity to claim he was ministering to them. While on my computer one day, I discovered he was surfing the web for pornography. He was having affairs with the young women he was counseling for years. I did not know it until God revealed it to me. The more and more he watched adult movies and websites, the more he started acting out the fantasies from them towards me that were formed in his mind. On some occasions, I didn't even want to have sex because he was so aggressive. First he denied and eventually he confessed but did not stop. He would pick arguments so I could put him out of the house to justify the affairs.

Everyone thought of us as "the perfect family". To keep peace, I hid his drug habits, his affairs, and the abuse from my friends, my family, and his family. He had this horrible side but was a remarkable father and person at times. He had become a Dr. Jekyll and Mr. Hyde; it would come and go. Time after time, he would apologize and promise that it would never happen again. I would hope that maybe this time would be different. Occasionally, he was the master of psychological manipulation. He loved to play games. When I had done something to displease him, real or imagined, he would ask about the incident in such a way as to make any answer seem extraordinarily out of pocket. The questions were almost rhetorical; yet, he always demanded an answer. My non-response infuriated him even more, usually resulting in aggressive verbal abusive or a threatening act. Victor often played these games with me and the children in slightly different forms tailored to our reactions.

At times, his control over me was increasing. He used threats and intimidation. When he felt he needed to take strong measures, he would grab me tightly or grab me by my neck. These occasions when he would snap and fly into a physically violent rage were actually rare compared to what one might imagine. They occurred on the average of every other month, although sometimes, more or less frequently. Before moving to Georgia, he was trying to impersonate a police offer and was arrested which resulted in him losing his job with the federal government. On this occasion, he was on a tyrannical rampage. The police was called and he was arrested and charged with domestic assault. He was convicted of the offense, placed on one-year probation, and mandated by the court to attend a Men's Domestic Violence Program. Somehow he managed to get by not having to complete the program. He lost his job because of his behavior. He blamed me for everything that was happening to him. Our financial situation was deteriorating, and I was very stressed out. He started to humiliate me and call me names. Finally, I called the police, he was arrested, and I filed for divorce.

The divorce was getting very ugly. He would use the court system as another avenue to abuse the family order of protection against him and fight to see the kids—even though the kids were sometimes terrified of him. He then used the court system as a way to abuse the family. He used the kids as pawns to pull me back into the cycle of abuse. After going in front of the judge for the divorce hearing, we had decided not to go through with the divorce because of financial reasons. After deciding not to divorce, I closed my hair salon and moved to Georgia. So after I moved, we reconnected.

Things seemed better for a while until his mood started again. Another incident happened. I did not deserve the abuse that I sustained. I was intensely emotionally and mentally tortured. We were on our way to New Jersey for our business. By this time, I had bought a home in Georgia. We were traveling back and forth for our business. We got into a heated discussion about our business affairs, our marriage, and how I managed our household finances. He admitted that was not something he liked to do. In the conversation, I disagreed with something he had stated. As usual, if I did not respond the way he wanted, he became abusive and insulting. He cursed me out, called me all kind of insulting names, and started road rage trying to run into other cars, speeding at 100 miles per hour. I was terrified! I begged and pleaded with him to stop. He eventually stopped. By this time I began to become so angry, I was seeking revenge. When he stopped alongside of the road to pee, I jumped into the driver's side and locked the door. My intention was to leave him alongside of the road, but he jumped on the side steps of the SUV and held on to the top rack as I drove down the highway. The police station was up ahead. Once I pulled into the station, I got out of the SUV and we both went inside. The officer asked, "What happened?" I explained to him what happened and that we have a history of domestic violence. He checked the history and let me go. I then separated from my husband for some time.

When we decided to reconnect again, one day I asked him, "Why do you get so angry?" He said, "I witnessed my step-father beating my mother."

He said that his step-father emotionally abused him and his mother. Through the years, I also learned my husband's biological father denied that he was his father. I attributed some of my husband's negative behavior to his dysfunctional family life but not the sexual perversion. Some of his patterns of behavior are attributed to his childhood. There were times in our marriage that he had no respect for me. He would call me some very explicit names in front of the children. I would ask him to leave. The next day, I would end up being the one who apologized.

In 2011, I was really going through it. I just found out my mother had died and to make things worse, my sister was diagnosed with breast cancer. He was not supportive at a time I really needed him. I was miserable and depressed. I was empty inside with shopping as my addiction. These things in my life reminded me of how empty I was. Victor and I argued even more and he became very distant. We separated again. I then found out that we were going to be grandparents. I was so happy at a time when I was going through so much pain. God does give us joy in the midst of pain! After several months, we got back together, but this time, he was worse than ever before. I found out he was having multiple affairs with younger women that I knew. When I confronted him, he started lying and manipulating. I asked him to leave and he became angry and charged at me. I told him it was over this time. I was done. He was trying to grab me, but our youngest son got between us. I managed to call the police and he was escorted with his clothes. He went back to New Jersey.

This was the final decision to end the abuse. We had been separated for over nine months. He pleaded that he made a mistake, he changed, and was sorry. He would make it up to us. All he wanted was to get his family back together and he would do whatever it took. He confessed to some of the affairs. He was convincing to me and those around him. I even gave him a 50th birthday party because I believed he had really changed and loved me. He started doing everything right, and I felt obligated to do my part to make our marriage work. But things got worse. Just like the other times, almost immediately, he was back to his cycle of abuse. He began to put a lock on his phone, claiming the devil was using me if I went through his phone. The tension started building and he began to mentally, emotional, and verbally abuse me to the point where I was emotionally drained. I found out he was still entertaining pornography, he was still conversing with the young ladies he had the affairs with. I decided it was over. He left and moved out. After him leaving, he believed as long as there was no actual physical violence, no domestic abuse had occurred. Of course, He blamed me!

After being married to Victor for over 27 years, I was able to gain an understanding that my abusive husband was not out of control; he chose to abuse me. In fact, it was during acts of abuse that he had the most power and control. Some people minimize the abuse that occurs and this can bring about doubts in those of us who experience the abuse. It's extremely important to remember that no one knows the situation as well as the victim.

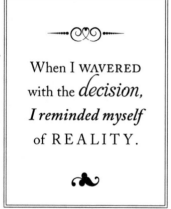

When I WAVERED with the *decision,* *I reminded myself* of REALITY.

Abuse is a pattern of behavior used to control another person. The abuse can be physical, emotional, verbal, social, or sexual. Non-physical abuse does not always result in broken bones, black eyes, or cuts and bruises. Emotional and verbal abuse can break a person's spirit and his or her confidence and self-esteem. Abusers can be found in every economic group, race, and ethnic group. They include those who live in million-dollar homes and people who live in poverty.

People often ask about women who were battered: "Why doesn't she just leave?" This is a natural question, but perhaps it would be wiser and more insightful to ask, "Why does he abuse?" The complicated and dangerous process of getting out entails many challenges that people who have never been battered may not consider. When I wavered with the decision, I reminded myself of reality. For me, reality included broken promises and unbearable pain inflicted by my husband. To help me with my decision, I weighed the risks. If I divorced him, it is very possible that I would remain single. If I stayed with this man, there is a very high probability that I would be abused again or dead.

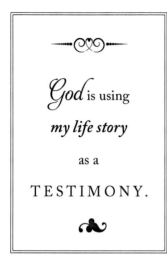

God is using

my life story

as a

TESTIMONY.

Loneliness will be a painful challenge. However, I choose to be alone and safe rather than living in fear and abuse. In retrospect, my loneliest times were when I was married to an abusive man. I lost this man as my husband, but gained safety, peace self-esteem, self respect, health, the return of my personality, and my life. I live with physical and emotional scars that will never go away but wake up every day knowing that God has set me free from the yoke of bondage!

The abuser must take responsibility for his or her actions. Without accepting accountability for it and wanting to work to replace abusive behaviors with healthy ones, abusive partners can't and won't make lasting changes. I know because my husband is still denying he has a problem and blames me for his actions. Even though I have suffered abuse, God is using my life story as a testimony. I hope anyone reading this can find strength to leave. You're not alone. You are fearfully and wonderfully made. God loves you just the way you are. One should ever have to endure domestic violence. Are you called out of your situation to speak out for such a time as this?

God has a purpose for you! He's called me to speak life into you.

The Spirit of the Lord is upon me, because he has anointed me to preach the gospel to the poor, he hath sent me to heal the broken hearted, to preach deliverance to the captives and recovering of the sight to the blind, to set liberty them that are bruised (Matthew 4:18).

My mission now is to advocate and to start a movement for reclaiming our voices and compelling others to hear us. I will utilize information and materials to educate

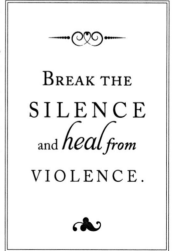

BREAK THE

SILENCE

and *heal from*

VIOLENCE.

and give resources for women, men, and children to empower. I also wish to give them a safe comprehensive outlet, visibility, and liberality to break the silence and heal from violence in their lives! Join me! Speak Out!

I shared my domestic violence story with you to assist, encourage, and inspire you and to bring hope! If we don't tell our stories, no one will know what domestic violence is like as it hides behind closed doors! "For God has not given us *(survivors)* the spirit of fear but of power, love, and a sound mind" (2 Tim 1: 7, emphasis mine).

Phaedra T. Anderson
Author: Developed in Darkness

Phaedra T. Anderson is a woman of God, encourager, poet, and writer. Her first book will be released in 2013. She has made contributions to the *Philadelphia Daily News, The Germantown Courier* and the following magazines: *Bronze, Women of Significance, Gospel 4 U, Beyond and motivateus.com.* You may reach her by email at phaedra.anderson@ yahoo.com or by phone at 267-230-0044.

STORY 8

DEVELOPED In Darkness

"God does some of His best work in the dark" is what I've learned while going through some of the darkest moments of my life. Many times I've felt as if I was living life with my eyes closed, unable to see anything around me. It was as if I was periodically placed in these dark rooms with the doors shut and then given instructions to "wait and listen" because if I was to come out too soon, I would be undeveloped and if I was to go by the things that I saw, I would become confused, because what you see and what you hear are not the same in darkness.

The first darkroom that I entered was called sickness. I will never forget it. It was gloomy. It was lonely and I was afraid. I had recently re-dedicated my life back to Christ. I was attending Bible Study classes during the week and I was at Sunday service faithfully. I can't quite explain it, but I started to thirst for the Word of God. I would even go to two services on fourth Sundays for our healing service.

WALK IN YOUR PURPOSE!

I'm not sure why I felt the need to go to our healing services. It wasn't like I was sick or anything. It just felt like somewhere that I needed to be. Later, I would find out why? But it was during those services that I really begun to open my mouth, to lift my hands, and give God praise.

> My *desire* to KNOW *God* was *INTENSE*. My *appetite* started to grow and I started to change.

The Word was rich, and I was really starting to understand what it meant to be a Christian and how important it was to develop a relationship with God. A relationship that I knew not of, but my pastor talked about the significance of this personal walk with the Lord, so much so, that I desired to have my own. It was that desire that kept me coming back, week after week. I just had to learn more about this God that wanted me to know Him in a very special way and the more I learned of Him, the more my life started to change.

My desire to know God was intense. My appetite started to grow and I started to change. Old relationships started to fade away, and I had enough strength to do what I wasn't able to do before. After eleven, long years of being in an unhealthy relationship, I was able to finally leave that man and move on with my life. Bad habits started to die. Hanging out in the clubs and going out to the bars were no longer of interest to me. My entire paradigm shifted, and I had a different outlook on how I viewed life as well as the way that I viewed myself, because it's impossible to sit under the uncompromising, unadulterated, life-giving Word of God and there not be a transformation. I had begun to change, so much so, that I didn't even want to have sex anymore outside of marriage. I started to see myself as God saw me. I was a woman of virtue and the more I heard the Word of God, the more the scales began to fall off my eyes and it was as if one day I woke up and said, "I don't want another man on top of me that is not my husband" and for the first time, as an adult, I felt pure. I felt renewed and I was happy within myself. I was actually becoming a new creature in Christ, and this new me was full of joy. Life was good and I was free. Free of emotional stress. Free of drama. Free of people and their expectations of me. I was just free and at peace within myself, and I was enjoying every bit of it.

Until one day, I was in the shower and while washing, I noticed a white, liquid discharge dripping out of one of my breast. At first I thought that I was seeing things, but when I squeezed my breast, this liquid fluid continued to drip out and when I squeezed the other one, the same thing happened. Now one may think that that's normal for some women, but it was not normal for me. Here I was, a 25-year-old woman without any children. There was no way that my breasts should have been leaking fluid. I was petrified because people were growing sick around me left and right, and every time I turned around, I was hearing that someone else had lupus or the "Big C". I panicked and immediately thought to myself that I had breast cancer, because that is what people usually do. We have one symptom and we become our own doctor and diagnose ourselves with the worst condition ever; and besides, what else could it have been?

I made a doctor's appointment and was sent to an endocrinologist. There I received the most shocking news of my life. The good news was that I didn't have breast cancer. The bad news was that after carefully examining my breasts, the doctor sent me away telling me that I could have a brain tumor and that I needed to have blood work done, immediately. He also proceeded to tell me that if the tests proved that there was a brain tumor present, they would have to go through my nose in order to operate on my brain. Leaving that doctor's office was one of the worst days of my life.

As I drove home, streams of tears were pouring down my face, as I saw my life flash before my eyes and what should have been a twenty minute drive… felt like forever. My mind was wandering at full speed, one hundred miles per hour and I couldn't turn it off. I could see my funeral. I could see myself lying in a casket. I could see myself dead and at every traffic light, all I heard in my ear was, "You have a brain tumor and you are going to die."

I cried all day and I cried all night for the first few days, because not only did I have the words of the doctor playing on instant replay in my head, but I also had this fluid leaking from my breasts which seemed to leak even more after I had received the doctor's report. I did not tell anyone because I didn't want anyone to worry, and I especially didn't want to worry my mom. She had already buried her youngest daughter, seventeen years prior. My mom, my five-year-old sister, and my eight-year-old cousin were walking across the street and were all hit by a drunk driver. I was eight-years-old at the time, and I remember going to the hospital and seeing my little sister laying in the hospital bed in a coma. The doctor said due to the trauma to her brain, she would never recover and would be a vegetable for the rest of her life. She stayed in a coma for almost two months, before my mom had to make one of the most difficult choices in her life, which was to pull the plug on her five-year-old daughter. Needless to say, my mom never really recovered from my sister's death.

So, I suffered in silence, which is what most people do when they first find out that they have some sort of sickness or disease, because with it comes shame and embarrassment, because you don't want people talking about you. You don't want people looking at you strange, and I even went as far as telling myself, "What's the point of telling people that can't help me anyway?" Not only could they not help, but they couldn't relate to me and I didn't want to hear, "I know how you feel" because they really didn't. They weren't the ones being faced with the possibility of having a brain tumor, and I really didn't want to hear, "It's going to be alright" because from the looks of it, it wasn't. My breasts were still leaking fluid and my tests were coming back positive. So I just kept it to myself and went to the only one that I knew could help me, Jesus.

I've heard of people getting mad at God and actually leaving the church when they fall sick, but that wasn't an option for me. Nor did it make sense. I mean, why would I leave my only source of hope? Man couldn't help me. Money couldn't help me. Only God could help me. So I continued attending church and I stayed enrolled in Bible Study, but often I would always ask God, "Why me?" and "Why now?" You would've thought that something like this would have happened when I was living out in the world. It wasn't supposed to happen after I've given my life to Christ. Or was it?

Weeks had gone by and my breasts were still leaking this milky fluid. My lab work came back positive and showed that I had an extremely high prolactin hormone level, which is what my doctor was concerned about, because high prolactin levels are the cause of a prolactin-secreting pituitary tumor on the brain. Typically, these tumors are non-cancerous and harmless, if they are caught in time, but at this point, we weren't sure of the size or the position of the tumor. When my doctor saw the results of the blood

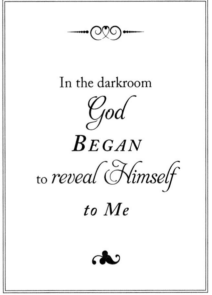

In the darkroom *God* **BEGAN** to *reveal Himself* *to Me*

work, he said that my prolactin level was so high that he was almost certain that I had a brain tumor, but he wanted me to take the test, again, to be sure. So, I did and as days went by and I continued to wait for the results, one evening while leaving out of Bible Study, I had begun to cry and asked God, "Why me?" and for the first time in my life, I heard the voice of God. He said, "Why not you? If I am a miracle worker and you need a miracle, why not you?" I can't explain how I knew, but everything in me knew that that was God and it was there, in that darkroom, that God would begin to reveal Himself to me.

At the time, I was working two jobs, pulling 60-70 hours a week, so I really didn't have much time to dwell on what was happening to me, which was a good thing. But there would be moments when I would be driving or during the midnight hour when it was just me and silence that I could tell you that fear and torment would try to overtake me. I would hear, "You have a brain tumor and you are going to die," but something was different. Fear and the threat of death didn't have the same impact on me anymore. For once I heard the voice of God, I never looked at my condition the same. God's voice rang in my ear louder than the voice of fear, and I had a made up mind that I wasn't leaving Jesus; if I was going to die, I was dying with him.

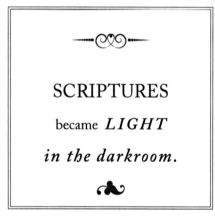

SCRIPTURES

became *LIGHT*

in the darkroom.

Before fluid even started leaking from my breasts, month after month, I would attend our healing services at church, take notes, and write down the scriptures, as my pastor would teach on the healing power of God. He would provide us with instructions on how to activate our faith and how faith, praise, and worship ushers in the presence of God and makes the atmosphere conducive for miracles. Often he would call prayer lines during these services and people would go to the altar that needed to be healed. You would see him laying hands on the sick and speaking healing into their bodies. I was so drawn to that atmosphere. You could literally see and feel the power of God at work, but never in a million years did I think that that power would be working in me. I had no idea that God was setting me up for a miracle in that darkroom.

Periodically, I would go back and review my notes that I had taken in church months back, and lo and behold, there were months of healing scriptures. Scriptures that I never thought that I would use, but they became light to me while in that darkroom. My breasts were still leaking fluid. My lab work was still coming back positive and I was still seeing death, but what I saw and what I heard was not one in the same because in my ear all I heard was: "By my stripes you are healed (1 Peter 2:24); It is the Lord thy God that healeth thee (Exodus 15:26); He sent forth his Word and healed them (Psalm 107:20); Many are the afflictions of the righteous, But the Lord delivers him out of them all" (Psalm 34:19). It was during this time that God's Word became real. It was no longer just words written on a piece of paper. In that darkroom, the Word of God became alive. It was there, that everything that I was learning Sunday after Sunday at church became relevant. So in my prayers I would declare and decree that my body was healed in Jesus' Name. I would speak those scriptures over my life and although my eyes still saw sickness, my ears heard healing.

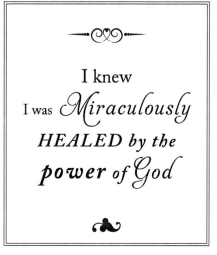

I knew I was *Miraculously* *HEALED by the* *power of God*

When I went back to the doctor's to get my results, the doctor had a strange look on his face. He said, "Ms. Anderson, your lab results are in conflict with one another. These levels are normal reflecting no sign of a tumor, but your other results were so high that it indicated that you had a tumor. They contradict one another so much that you will have to take a third test because I can't make a determination based on these two reports." I went back and got another test done and after the third test, my lab work showed that there was no sign of a tumor and my breasts had stopped leaking. I was then sent to have a CT-Scan for a fourth opinion, and that came back negative too. When my doctor called me back for a follow-up, his words to me were, "Ms. Anderson, I can't explain it, but all of your tests are now negative and there's nothing else that I can do for you. This goes to show that there is a God!" I left that room with tears streaming down my face, because I knew that I had been miraculously healed by the power of God.

That darkroom of sickness caused me to hunger and thirst after God all the more, because I didn't just know Him as Savior, but now I knew Him as Healer and that changed the entire dynamic of my relationship with Him. I would spend the next seven years of my life falling in love with Jesus.

It would be seven, long years before I would enter into another darkroom: the darkroom of "unemployment". It was lonely, uncomfortable, and filled with uncertainties. This room reminded me of a desert; for it was dry and barren. At the time, I worked for one of the major utility companies, in Philadelphia, as an executive coordinator. I supported one of the vice presidents' of the company and there were many perks associated with my position. Not only did I gross an excellent salary, had a good pension, along with great benefits, but I also had two company credit cards and since part of my job was to coordinate forums and meetings for C-level executives, I got to travel and stay at luxury hotels. I also ate at some of the best restaurants. I didn't have a need or a want in the world. I was single. I didn't have children and I was having it my way. I shopped until I dropped at Lord and Taylor and Saks Fifth Avenue were just a few of my best friends. I loved to travel and every year for my birthday, I would visit a different island by myself, just to enjoy God and his artwork. People would always ask how could I travel alone, but I never felt alone. My relationship with God had reached a level of intimacy that was far beyond words and those were times that He would just call me to Himself... away from the hustle and bustle of everyday life, away from the stresses of Corporate America, away from cell phones and technology, just away to be with His beloved. It was during those times that I would get instruction, clarification, assurance, confirmation, revelation, and direction for my life.

In 2008, my boss sold her house and moved to our Chicago office, and I was considering relocating as well. I always wanted to move out of the city and this seemed like the perfect opportunity, but when I went away to Jamaica in October 2008, I took it to the Lord and He said, "Wait". Nine months later, my entire department got laid off, including my boss, and we were all left unemployed. Just think, had I listened to people and had I not been in a position to hear God when he said, "Wait", I would've taken what looked to be the perfect opportunity and I would have been in Chicago without a job. However, when you acknowledge God in all of your ways, he will guide you and make your way straight (see Proverbs 3:5-

6). Needless to say, July 31, 2009, I was laid off after ten years of service, and my entire life changed as I entered into another darkroom.

For the first two years, I lived off of my severance, unemployment, and savings and through it all, I continued to tithe. Some may say that I couldn't afford to tithe for I was only living off of sixty percent of my salary, but I knew that I couldn't afford not to. So even while in my dry season, I tithed and I gave wherever God instructed me to. However, my funds were eventually exhausted and I no longer had an income, and within no time, I went from having it all to having nothing at all.

At first, it I didn't feel like a darkroom, but the longer I was in there, the darker it became. When I first got laid off, I was so happy because getting laid off allowed me to go after my dreams. I left with a good severance package and life was still good. I've always wanted to be a writer and to own a spa, and now I finally had the time to do both. I became a certified massage therapist, nail technician, and esthetician. I paid my tuition for school with a portion of my pension and I tried my best not to touch what was left of it, but it was impossible not to. The beauty field was slow and I didn't have enough clientele to sustain me financially. I tried to go back into the corporate world, but doors weren't opening, and that's when I started to feel the pressures of being in the darkroom. The world was in a recession. Jobs were far in between. Everyone around me was struggling just as much as I was, and again, all I was left to depend on was Jesus. For almost two years, I didn't have a source of income and it wasn't because I wasn't looking for a job, but the opportunities just weren't there. My monthly expenses amounted to two-thousand dollars a month. Now how was I supposed to live off of no income?

I had a lot of time on my hands and most of it was spent doing volunteer work, writing, and praying. I now had time to socialize on social networks. I met new people and by the click of a button, my work was beginning to get recognition and my articles would be published in three different magazines. Who would have thought that my writing career would be launched in a darkroom? There were many times that I couldn't feel God, but I could see him working behind the scenes. Prayer was a necessity. I would spend hours laying before God and reading my Bible. Those two things ultimately got me through. I feasted on the Word and "Man shall not live on bread alone, but on every word that comes from the mouth of God" (Matthew 4:4) became my portion. I spent very little time watching television because on every channel was coverage of the recession and how there weren't any jobs. So that was just not what I needed to hear. I didn't want to feed my fears, so I stayed in the Word of God and fed my faith. I wrote in my journal a lot, because although I was in a darkroom and I couldn't see my today from my tomorrow, I could still hear God and I would hear him say things like, "Trust Me. I will never leave you or forsake you" (see Hebrews 13:5) and "The just shall walk by faith" (Habakkuk 2:4).

Fear ruled me in the other darkroom, but not in this one. My experiences with God and my prayer life had shot me to a place where fear couldn't go, but the uncertainty of not knowing when and how my daily needs would be met left me uncomfortable. Month to month I had no idea how my bills were going to get paid. I worked short-term temp assignments just to pay a bill or two. Things were tight. One month, I had to pawn most of my jewelry just to pay my rent. I was so embarrassed. After receiving the money, I left out, got in my car, and I just sat there with tears streaming down my face. I couldn't believe that this was happening to me. I had literally hit rock bottom, but you would had never known by looking at me. God never allowed me to look like where I was. I was in a place of lack, but I still drove a Lexus and my appearance never changed. I was literally making it off of the grace, mercy, and favor of God, because although my bills were stacked up, I never got an eviction notice. I never spent one day in the dark or the cold, and my car never got repossessed.

Resources were so scarce that I found myself applying for public assistance. I've been working since I was sixteen-years-old. Never have I been on welfare and there I was 34-years-old applying for food stamps. You talk about felling mortified! But I didn't see any other way because I was going by what I saw and not by what I heard, because what I heard was "The Lord thy God shall supply all of your needs" (Philippians 4:19), but what I saw were empty cupboards. One morning, I swallowed my last ounce of pride and I went to the welfare office. I was standing, there full of shame, and I heard the Lord say, "This is not for you." Immediately, with tears rolling down my eyes, I left before they even called my name, and I got in my car and went home. Later that day, I got a call from my cousin and she said, "I just ran into seven hundred and fifty dollars, and half of it is yours." There was the money that I needed for food and from that point on, God would reveal Himself to me as Jehovah Jireh, the Lord that provides.

I would see God provide for me in miraculous ways in that darkroom. I received unexpected checks in the mail for thousands of dollars. I had a case in deliberation for years that finally made settlement, and not only did I get one financial settlement, but I was blessed with two settlements. I walked away from the table with two checks totaling $14,000, and even now, God is still providing for me in this darkroom. Though I sit here with many uncertainties, there's one thing that I am certain about and that is "the Lord will provide." I still don't have permanent employment, but God is still making ways out of no way.

I've been working as a temporary employee for the last five months and just after two months of working for the company, I was talking to Ms. Kathy, one of the permanent employees there. I shared with her my desire to participate in Dr. Lily's writing project as a contributing-author for this book, Walk in Your Purpose. Never in a million years did I think that she would have a fundraiser and God would touch the hearts of the people within that company, from the vice president to the customer service representatives, to donate money to cover the cost for me to tell my story and let others know that they are not alone in the darkrooms of life.

So, I know how it feels to be in a darkroom for I am writing in the dark. My employment as a temp can end today or tomorrow. I am still trying to start a business and pursue my dream as a writer with limited resources. I see that I don't have any health benefits. I see that my money is still funny. However, I hear, "Your God shall supply all of your needs" (Philippians 4:19). I hear, "It is the Lord, thy God that gives you power to produce wealth" (Deuteronomy 8:18). So as you see, what I see and what I hear are complete opposites, and although both are realities, I have chosen to lean on what I hear and wait in His Word. But as I wait in this darkroom, I know that there are others waiting too, and I come to encourage you, because negatives are always developed in darkrooms, and it is in these rooms that God is doing some of his best work. It is in this place where God is perfecting you. It is in this place where God is establishing you. It is through these circumstances that God is building your faith and teaching you how to trust him. It is during these moments that God authenticates your call and purpose in life. It is right here, in darkness, where God strengthens and prepares you to walk into your purpose. It is here, in the darkrooms of life, where God develops us and we go from negatives, which no one is able to make out, to beautiful pictures that bring God glory!

Be encouraged in your darkroom because you will come out a perfect picture.

Marita DeMarinis
Author: Through the Valley to the Mountain Top

Marita DeMarinis of Chicago, Illinois, is passionate about being the voice for the voiceless. She is a member of New Life Covenant Church, the Director of A Poem to the King-Poetry Ministry, is employed as a Workforce Coordinator at a local non-profit agency, and is an avid animal lover. You may contact Marita by email at marita_demarinis@ yahoo.com or call 773-960-6971.

STORY 9

Through the Valley to the Mountain Top

It is a cold, wintery, Chicago Wednesday night, January 9th, 2013 at 10:09 pm, Arturo's 24 Hour Mexican Restaurant. I finally sit, am still, and am writing the first page of my story. The Lord has used my pastor, Pastor Wilfredo De Jesus of New Life Covenant Church, a church for the hurting to speak the message of writing my story in a book or devotional on numerous occasions. The first time Pastor said this directly to me four years ago, and lastly this past Sunday in his message on "What is My Purpose"? He spoke on how God allows trials and tribulations to refine our character to grow us from the test to the testimony, and that in your valley experience, there may a book in the making. Without that valley experience, that book may have never been written.

As I sit in the same booth, in the same restaurant that I have literally soaked my pages with tears as I have written many of my poems of the past. Tonight, I am not crying, but eagerly writing from the depth of my soul because I have a story to tell. My story, my pain, my trials, my failures, my deliverance, God's love, God's protection, God's restoration, God's redemption, and God's perfect will, plan and purpose for my life.

Hence, here is my story. The story of Marita…from the valley of despair to the mountain top of hope, encouragement, and provision.

"My world came crashing down on June 17, 2006, the day my father passed away. Everything changed that day—the day before Father's Day. My world the way I once knew it was no longer…my reality a distant fantasy. At that very moment of his death, his last breath, I realized I didn't have any family. My life eternally altered forever. My holidays would never be the same. Where would I go? Who would I be with? Alone is now my new best friend." -Excerpt from "Father's Day" –A poem by Marita DeMarinis.

The sting of his death hit me like a ton of bricks, like no other loss I have ever experienced. I loved my dad, a man who raised me as his own, although he was not my biological father. You would have thought I was his. We had the same nose; we looked alike and had the same drive in life. Some things in life were not genetic. He taught me how to see a goal and make it happen with hard work, discipline, and determination. He was a former Golden Gloves Champ that attended Rocky Marciano's training camp in the late 1940's and he was a decorated Expert Marksman Marine. He had an adventurous, competitive, trailblazing spirit. He would somehow manage to convince me to go skydiving with him, jumping out of a commuter plane, free falling with no guide as they do today or to ride a 100-mile century bike ride in a very mountainous Lake Tahoe terrain. As I rode my bike up the first hill, I kept thinking to myself, if I can't even get up the first hill how am I going to finish this entire race? I always remember him simply saying, "This isn't a hill; this is a mountain. Do whatever it takes. Walk your bike to the top, but keep going. We need to finish this race." Ironically enough, the first mountain was actually the biggest mountain of the whole ride. If I would have quit, I would have never known that the other mountains and hills were much easier to climb and finish the race. Little did I know at the time, how important his message was for me and my life after this ride. He spoke wise words that day that I would later reflect on in the midst of my valley experiences. It was when I was at the lowest of lows, I would truly miss him. I would remember how he would have his café at midnight, go to bed, and be up five hours later, café in hand. He was always my encourager, my cheerleader, my teacher. He was far from perfect, had his flaws, but I knew he loved me.

The following months after my father's funeral were like a fog. I was drunk at the funeral, and drank almost daily thereafter; I somehow managed to function at work, but couldn't concentrate. I was grieving my father, but also mourning the break-up of my boyfriend who chose to go to a baseball game rather than to attend my father's wake. My life was in chaos and just seemed to go from bad to worse. God had a unique way of getting my attention through this gut wrenching, painful sting of death.

My Heavenly Father knew how much I loved my earthly father. He used my father's death to get my attention through the intense anguish I felt. He revealed to me it was not only in the time of death that I drank. I drank to cope with life in general. I had been drinking on a regular, consistent basis for over 15 years. God revealed to me the exact source of my pain.

It was rejection from the time I was born and unwanted, to being placed up for adoption, to a violation of rape in school, to several failed relationships with unavailable men who were not capable of a healthy, loving relationship. God used my father's death ultimately to bring me to my knees, to acknowledge that Jesus was my Lord and Savior, to become an eternally adopted daughter of Christ into the Kingdom of Heaven. I gave my life to the Lord on September 18th, 2006. I stopped drinking October 12, 2006; I have been sober ever since by the grace of God's hand and was baptized December 31st, 2006. It was in the storm and the stillness of the storm that God revealed one truth after another to me. When God has a mission for us to accomplish, we must realize that it is in His exact and precise timing. The day after I got baptized, God had given me the ability to write my first poem. I had never written poetry prior to this monumental day. It was a new gift from my heavenly Father. It was my first holiday season alone, and God gave me this beautiful gift of poetry! It was a tool for me to express the tremendous pain that I was going through, to cry my pain through my paper and my pen, and later on to worship God through my poems and rhyme.

For the next 6 years, it was constant state of complete loss and despair. I lost my dad, I lost my boyfriend. I lost four jobs in four years, and I lost my house and seven of my properties. I lost my car, and at times, I felt like I lost my mind. My things were put out on the street like garbage, and people walked away and took my belongings. There is something very humbling when you have no control of your entire life, finally acknowledge that God is in control of absolutely everything! I remember asking God to help me find three things after my things were put in the street: my Bible, my flute and my mother's recipes. I told God that if He let me find my flute, I will play it unto the Lord. I had played my flute since I was in the 5th grade and had a collection of sheet music. My music was gone. God would have to give me the gift to play prophetically. I was able to find my Bible and my flute. God eventually did give me the gift to play my flute prophetically and the opportunity to play for His Kingdom. I never found my mother's recipes.

I went through a wide range of emotions, from anger and depression... asking God, "Why me? What did I do to deserve this?" I kept asking why? I had to guard my heart to whom I spoke to about my situation. So many times Christian folks want to be the first to point the finger about the reason you may be having a storm in your life. They automatically think you are in sin, rather than God having a divine purpose and plan for your suffering. Careful church...

> *Do not judge, or you too will be judged. For in the same way you judge others, you will be judged and with the measure you use, it will be measured to you (Matthew 7:1-2 NIV).*

> *Consider it pure joy, brother, when you face trials of many kinds, because you know that testing of your faith develops perseverance. Perseverance must finish its work so that you may be mature and complete, not lacking anything (James 1:2-3 NIV).*

I would read these scriptures daily in addition to the Book of Job, who was a man in the Bible who lost his family and his fortune. God later restored Job's family and fortune in his later years because God was and still is a restorer.

My lifestyle had changed. Although I wasn't raised with money and was raised very modestly, there was a period of time in my adult life when I thought I had "made it". I lived well without having to worry about money while I was employed as a United States Probation Officer with the government. Funny how things can change quicker than you can blink an eye. In December 2007, I resigned from my government job and wanted to try the non-profit sector in my field of counseling that I officially had never utilized the master's degree that I worked so hard to obtain. Never did I anticipate the 2008 recession, crash of the housing market, accelerated foreclosures, and unemployment rates at an all time high for the next four years. As I attempted to work in the non-profit sector, I was laid off four times within four years for various budget cuts. I made a decision to return to my old neighborhood—a three-block melting pot of Italians, Mexicans, and Puerto Ricans in the midst of the city. At least I knew that I would be able to find an apartment based on who I knew rather than a credit check that I knew I couldn't pass.

My Link card became like my former Golden American Express Card. I now was the recipient of services that I used to refer clients to in my former life of employment in social services. I was now the low income client who now applied to live in public housing. I went to my church's food pantry, I applied for heat and light assistance to cover my winter bill, I paid the landlord in cash and many times even in quarters. I was so depressed that I didn't open my mail for one year. I pawned my jewelry and my father's ring. I was attempting to survive, at times, barely existing, but still managing to get to service twice a week, crying my heart to the Lord! Reminding God of His Word that "He would never leave me or forsake me," even if the world turned it's back on me. I was still living, breathing, waking up every day even when the clouds were grey. God was doing a work in me.

Although, I had some savings at the time I had resigned, that quickly was depleted in my attempt to save my seven properties that were going to foreclosure status at an accelerated pace. I had jokingly stated that if this was the benefit to coming to know the Lord, what was it like if He really liked you? During this time period, I would describe it as the loneliest time of my entire life. I had never felt so alone, with no family or anyone to count on. In the midnight hour, when I would cry myself to sleep, my puppy, Gizmo, would always kiss my tears in his way to console me. I also had two other puppies, Buffy and Vinnie, who were part of God's plan to help me cope and get through the tough times. God knew He gave me these puppies because I would have to get up, let them out, and take them for a walk three times a day, rather than sleep the day away. He knew when my heat was cut off, that it would be my puppies that would cuddle with me to stay warm. I remember when I truly hit my bottom the day I came home and the heat was off. I could see my breath in the air, and my puppies were shivering. I just felt like such a failure that I couldn't even take care of my dogs, let alone myself. That night, I put their little puppy coats on, we all cuddled under a blanket, and I prayed to God to not let us feel cold throughout the night. God heard my prayers. Somehow we all feel asleep and the heat by the hand of God came on! Praise Him!

There were still days I couldn't even get out of bed. I continued to struggle with depression that would overwhelm me. As my struggle seemed to get stronger, I still abstained from alcohol. I truly was living life on life's terms: the true reality of sobriety at its best by the grace of God. I just couldn't believe that this is where I was with my life—no husband, no baby, no family, no job, no nothing. I was struggling; all I had was my faith in God that at times even wavered. However, God would always provide me a way, with the loving church family that I was very cautious to embrace for fear of being hurt or rejected. I was so glad to be part of a church whose mission was that we were a church for the hurting. God was teaching me that I indeed did have a family who loved and cared for me! It was my family in Christ, who would pray for me, bring me groceries, help with my rent that was months in arrears, give me a seven day bus pass, offer me a ride home after service in the extreme heat or cold of the Chicago weather, invite me for holidays or dinner, and even have a birthday party for me.

God didn't want to me focus on my hardship; he wanted to be praised during this ongoing storm of my life. God was telling me step up and help someone else who was worse off than me! This is when I truly grasped the concept that "it wasn't about me". It was in my lowest of low that I actually was utilized in a very strong way for the Lord. God showed me the scripture better than he could tell me: "My grace is sufficient for you, for my power is made perfect in weakness" (2 Corinthians 12:9 NIV). This scripture meant that when I was at my weakest breaking point, God would give me the power to do things in His name that I was not capable of doing on my own power. It was in my weakness that God's glory was revealed. I remember one day I was to teach a lesson in my recovery group. I had just lost my job earlier that day. I was clearly upset about losing my job; however, it never occurred to me not to go teach my lesson. That is how I knew God's presence in my struggle and a peace that surpassed all of my understanding; I was going to be alright. It was not by my hand that I delivered that lesson; it was only through the power of the Holy Spirit that I could speak with clarity and deliver a precise, powerful lesson on the topic of surrender, nonetheless. God has humor and jokes, just in case you didn't know!

God was teaching me how to receive love, how to receive help, how to stay humble, and never forget where I come from. I was truly learning that God loves and cares about me. During this time, I was the Jill of all trades and had returned to working in the Italian restaurant that I was raised working in since I was 10-years-old. God had to take me back to the beginning of being a dishwasher, waitress, and cleaning lady. There was no shame in my game; I needed to work and did what I had to do. I needed to be around people because my natural instinct was to isolate. I finally had to surrender to God during our church's cooperate fast in January 2013 and told Him finally, "If You want me to be a waitress, I will be content and be a waitress," as

> *God was teaching me how to receive love, how to receive HELP, HOW TO STAY humble.*

this was a very honorable and hard-working profession. Prior to this, I had become frustrated because I simply could not find another job, despite the fact that I constantly applied for them. God is awesome! Within two weeks of my final surrender to Him regarding my employment situation, I received two job offers at the same time. This had never happened to me. Ironically enough, I declined the higher paying job and went with my current position of being a Workforce Coordinator. In this job, I help other people find jobs. I love my job! My hardship of the last seven years has led to my calling. I had to go through what I went through to get where I am and where I am going. The process was not easy; it was painful but necessary. God has orchestrated every single step of my book of life.

Out of my trials, God was glorified on every single account: my poetry ministry was birthed, A Poem to the King, which were poems composed that couldn't have been written unless I went through the storm. I was the first Christian poet to advance into the finals of a prestigious secular poetry event in Chicago, the Gwendolyn Brooks Open Mic Award. I came in second place. My Christian poetry glorifying God has been published in secular journals several times. I have been able to recite Christian poems to other secular institutions in Chicago, the University of Chicago, Printer's Row, Harris Theater, art exhibits, and numerous summer events in the city. In addition, I completed a two year School of Ministry program, became a part of the church choir, and now teach poetry at the my church's transitional home called the Chicago Dream Center for woman with addiction, homelessness, and prostitution issues. I have been riding the bus for two years since my car was taken from me. This has given me an opportunity to minister and witness to others while waiting for the bus or while riding the bus. I was making the most of every opportunity. I finally had learned to praise God for who He is and not what He could do for me. I had to get the focus off my struggle and keep my focus on serving God and keeping Him first in my life! I learned the aspect of what being a servant of God really was in action and not just in word, even while my storm raged.

God allowed me to go through the valley because I had to go through it to get to the mountain top. There were so many blessings that came

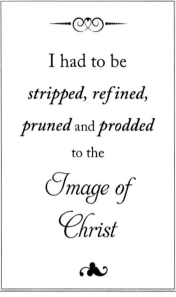

> I had to be
>
> *stripped, refined,*
>
> *pruned* and *prodded*
>
> to the
>
> *Image of*
> *Christ*

out of the seven years of pruning and purging that simply would have not been possible if I was still making $75,000 dollars at my government job and had all of my properties. When I had all of those material things and distractions, I didn't have time for God. My focus was not on loving and serving people; it was on me. When I was so busy working from 8:30 in the morning until 9:00 at night, there was not a creative bone in my body.

God knew exactly what He was doing when he allowed the trials and tribulations that had occurred in my life over the last seven years. This was part of His divine plan for my life. I had to be stripped, refined, pruned, and prodded to the image of Christ. I constantly had to die to the flesh of my desires and will… fervently praying and fasting for God's will and desire to be present in my life. I had to renew my mind daily, through reading and studying His Word and fellowshipping with other believers.

God has given me rest in the 7th year of this journey! Although, this year is not even half over, God has filled my life with favor. He has given me peace and purpose. He has given me a job that I have passion for and a message to those who are unemployed. He has opened doors that no man could have ever opened. God is a restorer, and as we speak, He is bringing restoration and order back to my life. The year 2013 is my Walk in Purpose in serving God and his people through my writings and with helping others on their journey to purpose and employment. I have seen the valley of despair, and I continue to keep climbing to the mountain top. This doesn't mean I don't have challenges or struggles. Ladies, quitting is not an option, keep climbing the mountain. You will never see the mountain top if you stop now. To God be all the Glory!

Nathalie Jones, MSW, PhD
Author: Out of Order

Nathalie "Passion" Jones, MSW, PhD is a Christian, wife, mother, educator, and a loyal person to everyone that she meets. Nathalie is the founder of PASSION for life coaching that focuses on empowering women and girls. Her hobbies includes: reading, empowering and encouraging women to reach their maximal potential in life. You may contact Nathalie through her website: www.passionforlifecoach.com or by calling: 682-667-5484.

STORY 10

Out of Order

To everything there is a season, a time for every purpose under heaven:
Ecclesiastes 3:1 (NKJV)

I decided to turn in a little early one night while staying in the hospital room. It was cold, quiet, and very dark along the hallways. First, I was feeling nervous because I was not in a familiar place, but I eventually allowed myself to drift off. Then, all of a sudden, my husband and I were driving in our car along a highway through very steep mountains. I was in the passenger seat and decided to look behind me out of the back window. During that time, I saw cars that were wrecking and piling up on one another. Also, I saw huge rocks falling from the top of the mountains, and it appeared that the series of wrecks were approaching our vehicle. As the rocks became closer to our car I turned around to see what was in front of us and all of a sudden everything became dark.

Then, I started to reflect over my life and realized I was broken down, jobless, hopeless, homeless and helpless. According to Paul in I Corinthians 14:40, "Let all things be done decently and in order" (NKJV).

Life without order is similar to sliding down a steep hill at a fast pace while passing people, places and things without the ability or willingness to stop.

PHASE ONE: CHILD OUT-OF-ORDER

Order is the freedom from disruption or disorder that is held together by systems (Trimm, 2007). The systems included my relationships, career and religious paths. My life appeared to be out of order since conception. My mother was sixteen, my grandparents were raising me and my relationships with my uncles were as though we were siblings. My household responsibilities have always included: extensive chores, baby-sitting my siblings, and ultimately taking on a full-time care giving role to my siblings at some point of my life. My life continued down a path of parenting, acting as both male and female in relationships, and unaware that I was out of order.

I am the eldest child of my mother; my parents conceived me when they were in high school. Therefore, I was conceived out of order and raised in the home of my maternal grandparents. Rather than going on play dates or playing with dolls, I attended business meetings with my grandmother and was involved in several community organizations with her. I was known as the little girl that had a large amount of wisdom and knowledge.

Fast forwarding to high school, I started dating a gentleman that I thought was perfect for me. School was very low on his priority list, but I felt that he could be successful if he could just apply himself. The longer I dated him, the more teachers, coaches and friends felt he was not the guy for me. My parents never knew this, but I would take the school bus from the same neighborhood that he lived in, get to school, borrow my friend's car to return home, and pick him up from school. I would help him with homework, rides to work. I would go totally above and beyond although knowing that he was unmotivated and unwilling to make strides to pursue personal or professional success.

I had no idea that my life had become unmanageable—in that I was out of order and living my life as an adult as early as six years of age.

PHASE TWO: YOUNG ADULT OUT-OF-ORDER

After my first year of college, my high school boyfriend came to see me when he completed basic training for the military. When he stepped off of the plane, he greeted me with a ring and asked me to marry him. Due to his military status, we were allowed to have a marriage ceremony on the spot, so we did. We totally eloped; we went to the courthouse in our matching jean wear. He had on his jean shorts and a white shirt and I had on my jean dress with a white shirt. I was 18 year of age and a wife without understanding the true responsibilities of this role.

The marriage was short lived and consisted of more wrong than right on my part. At this point in life, I have taken full responsibility for jumping into that role for personal gain. I was thriving for my perception of "the family life" and therefore, out of order while pursuing that goal. During this phase, I withdrew from college, relocated, and stopped playing basketball to be a full-time wife. I continued to make one poor choice after the next in areas such as spirituality, relationships, and finances.

According to Trimm (2007), this was known as a viscous cycle of failures and defeat that I was not aware of. A few years later I met a new gentleman that was interested in offering me his friendship. He said, "I have been watching you and I have noticed that you don't smile very much." Every day that I spent time with this gentleman, he made conscious efforts to make jokes and take walks with me. I felt as though I had smiled more than I ever had in my lifetime. There were embarrassing times when he would make jokes and I became defensive because I was unclear that it was in fact a joke.

During this time, I had full custody of my younger brother. He was involved in extracurricular activities at the local high school and I was in my last year of college and starting a new relationship. I had not realized that I was in over my head; I felt like I was doing what needed to be done. I would go to school in the morning, work in the afternoons, and attend my brothers sporting events during the evening. I had clearly underestimated the meaning of doing things in order.

What order is this: a college student, early twenties, full-time employee, raising my brother, married then divorced, and now down a road of starting a new relationship?

PHASE THREE: ADULT LIFE OUT-OF-ORDER

Now that my life seemed to have one complication after the next, I learned that I was expecting my first baby—out of wedlock. When I went into labor, I drove myself to the hospital, parked my car in visitor's parking, and labored my baby girl. When the hospital clerks released us to return home, I drove us to the Walgreens drive through to pick up prescriptions and home we went. The gentleman that wanted to make me laugh lived oversees for work, but made it his business to remain in close contact with me. One summer when he came to visit, we decided to read *Purpose Driven Life* by Rick Warren. After reading it, we decided that we wanted and needed to get married rather than live a sinful lifestyle. On July 21, 2007, we became husband and wife, and I was definitely displaying some of the same behaviors from my first marriage. I was protecting, parenting, and trying to provide for a man that did not need those things. During our earlier days, I can remember a disagreement that we had because I became overwhelmed in my responsibilities as a wife and mother. He looked at me in my eyes and said, "You won't let me do anything." He said, "You won't give me information to pay bills, you won't allow me to go grocery shopping, and you won't give me the keys to check the mailbox." I was totally embarrassed, but I didn't know how to change my controlling, caretaking, and overall crazy behaviors. At that point, I was working several jobs, making all of the decisions, and resolving all of the issues that would arise.

"Whoever offers praise glorifies me; And to him who orders his conduct aright I will show the salvation of God" (Psalm 50:23, New King James Version).

In 2009, my life started to spin out of control. The obstacles that were somewhat under control had increased. They felt similar to the Florida winds of a hurricane as it picked up strength. During this year, I miscarried and had to spend several months out of work in a full-time capacity. Eventually, I lost my job and when I returned for my 10-week check-up, I had a flickering light under the ultrasound; I was pregnant again. During the pregnancy I took on several teaching positions. It was my thought that I needed to provide for our family alone.

In 2010, I gave birth to our baby boy and I was still walking out of order. I increased my work load and spent many days and nights in front of the computer screen trying to earn pay checks. When bills were due, I would call for extensions and borrow money to make sure that our house would stand. It was so intense that my husband would start making comments that I needed to put the computer away. I felt that I had to work in order for us (the family) to eat and live. There were many times that I would be present in the body but absent from the mind because I was always thinking about how I was going to protect, provide, and parent everyone in the house including my husband.

It was evident today that the Lord was screaming at me to seek order all along.

Phase Four: Out-of-Order

In 2011, I actually tuned in to hear the Lord's whispers. I was speaking on the phone to a friend, and I was describing all of the things that I needed to do for the house. For instance, I was discussing that I needed to pay a few bills, take the car to the shop, take the kids shopping, and contact the landlord for a payment extension. My friend was very soft spoken. She said to me, "Nathalie, you are out of order." I was stunned and had a blank stare on my face! I did not know how to respond. She explained that God provides order to everything. She mentioned there is a time for everything, a time to be born, and a time to die (Ecclesiastes 3:1). She said, "You are all over the place and need to get yourself together." She suggested that I read a book called *The Power of a Whisper: Hearing God and Having the Guts to Respond* by Bill Hybels. She said, "You need to learn to hear from God and to follow His Word." I was very embarrassed because I did not know that I was out of order or that I was supposed to get in order. So, day by day, I delved into this book so I could learn to hear God's whispers and have the

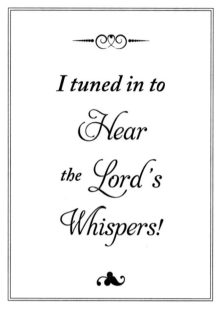

I tuned in to Hear *the* Lord's Whispers!

guts to respond (Hybels, 2009).

Although she has shared this information about order, I was unclear on how to change my behaviors. So, I decided that I needed to do a fast so that I could become closer to the Lord and to be able to hear His whispers. This was the most God-centered and clear time of my life. On the day after I ended my fast, my son suffered with second and third degree burns on his face and shoulders. It was a horrible day that started off so lovely and turned into chaos. My son and I stayed in three hospitals in two states and three cities over a seven-day period. Additionally, he had countless surgeries and he was only 13-months-old. While in the hospital caring for him, I was calling bill collectors and making payment arrangements. Our electricity was turned off twice; we were down to one car, and trying to keep gasoline in it. Our mortgage was past due, and I was borrowing funds to keep us from losing our home. I never stopped to think whether I was in order because a crisis took place, and I remained in a comfortable role that consisted of caretaking to the full extent.

PHASE FIVE: GOD'S WHISPERS OF ORDER

One day, when I was in the hospital with my son, I was reading the book about tuning into God's whispers. The book mentioned how one must be still and allow the words of God to manifest in his heart and in his mind. So, I decided to sit in silence at the hospital and tuned in to God. What I heard was, "You are out of order; the time is now for you to stand down and allow your husband to head his household." It was so clear and when I opened my eyes, I had tears drifting down the sides of my face as though I had released something.

In that moment I knew that I had to make a change and that God was going to put me to the test to see whether I truly trusted Him.

The next night, I decided to turn in a little early while staying in the hospital room. It was cold, quiet, and very dark along the hallways. First, I was feeling nervous because I was not in a familiar place, but I eventually allowed myself to drift off. Then, all of a sudden, my husband and I were driving in our car along a highway through very steep mountains. I was in the passenger seat and then I decided to look behind me out of the back window. During that time, I saw cars that were wrecking and piling up on one another. Also, I saw huge rocks falling from the top of the mountains, and it appeared that the series of wrecks were approaching our vehicle. As they became close to our car, I turned around to see what was in front of us and all of a sudden everything went dark..... . I had fallen asleep and needless to say, I woke up gasping for air and feeling scared out of mind. Although I was not clear of what that dream meant, I knew that God was trying to speak to me.

It was after this daunting, yet vivid dream that I sought wise counsel for clarity of the dream. I was told that God was showing me that everything around me was crumbling, shattering, and ultimately, a total wreck. But I needed to continue to move forward knowing that if I trust in God that he will direct my path. Of course I was on a high alert because I was expecting my life to become totally chaotic.

I placed a call to my husband to let him know that the electricity was turned off while he was at work. I had them turned back on before he came home. I informed him that the car insurance had expired; therefore, we were no longer covered. I also stated that the baby would need several surgeries due to his injury. And I shared that our mortgage was several months late and I think that we were about to lose our home. I did a complete purge in order to allow my husband to take over his leadership role. I felt that I was instructed by God and had to remove the pressure from my chest. Although I knew that my husband could not make miracles happen in these areas, it felt good to share this information rather than protecting him from his role as the provider and protector of our home. I had now started to engage him in the series of our life that he deserved to be a part of.

I Wanted to

Walk in Order

KNOWING

God

will supply

all of our needs.

When the baby and I arrived home from the hospital after one of his surgeries in December, there was a judgment (eviction letter) on the door that said we had to be out by January 1, 2012. When he arrived, I shared the paperwork with him. My aunt wanted to give me the money to take care of the situation, but I declined. I shared with her that my husband will let me know what route he would like for us to take. I had girlfriends that wanted us to move in with them. But I continuously shared with them that my husband will make the decisions for us. I remember that my cousin and best girlfriends thought that I was totally losing my mind. But I wanted to walk in order knowing that God will supply all of our needs. My walk with the Lord has been strengthened and I had a new stride in my walk.

My husband suggested that we pray and take a few days to hear from the Lord. I was in shock because I never knew that my husband could pray in such of a profound manner, and I never allowed him to show his ability to lead us. On December 28, he and I sat on the steps of our home, with our hands held and tears in our eyes. I felt like we both knew that our life was about to take on a new shape. He was sitting on the higher step holding my hand below him and pulled me up to him for a hug. He told me that we were going to get through this, and it was so comforting to have a partner rather than carrying the load alone. I could clearly see that my steps were ordered by God.

PHASE SIX: WALKING IN ORDER

My husband looked me in my eyes and said, "This is your dream." We are going to have to leave everything behind us because it is crumbling, and we need to start over. My heart was broken on the inside; I wanted so bad to hang on to our life in Florida. We were leaving our church, family, friends and careers. For sure, we were living beyond our means and barely making it from month to month, but it was apparent that our time had run out. If we were willing to trust God, He was going to start us "anew".

He took my hand and said, "We are going to sell everything out of our house and move to Texas." He said, "I spoke with my friend and he is going to allow us to stay in their home until we are capable of finding our own." God had already worked it out. Although, I was frightened out of my mind, I trusted in God to give my husband the wisdom and knowledge that he needed to get us through this time.

On January 1, we were homeless. We had an air mattress, our car, our children, and friends that allowed us to stay in their home for two weeks.

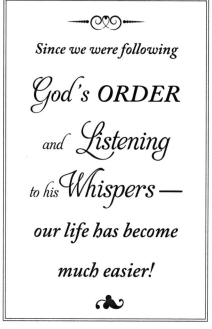

Since we were following God's ORDER *and* Listening *to his* Whispers — *our life has become much easier!*

It was then that we drove to Texas carrying only our clothes, a few small, special items, and a small amount of cash in our pockets. In fact, once we reached the Dallas County city limits, we had enough money for one more fill-up of gasoline. Since we were in following God's order and listening to his whispers, our life has become much easier. Upon arrival, we were greeted with an envelope of cash to start us on our way. Additionally, the doorbell rung and when I opened the door, there were approximately forty bags at the door full of toiletries for my family and me. But God! He had sent an angel to welcome us and to encourage us to continue to trust in

Him. By the third week, my husband had a full-time job, I had a full-time job, the kids were thriving, and six months later, we had our own place to call home.

Order brought significant change in our life that has led us to a more peaceful place.

PHASE SEVEN: LIFE WITH OR WITHOUT ORDER

ORDER
brought significant
CHANGE
which led us to a
Peaceful
Place

I had several roles during my lifetime, but most of them consisted of caretaking. Although I thought that I was doing the right thing, biblically, I was not. God displayed examples of order early in the Bible. For instance, he made Adam first in his own image and then Eve to be fruitful and multiply. I am thankful that God saw my heart and my willingness to seek order and the manner that he guided my husband to put us in an atmosphere that we could thrive as a family.

Historically, I was raised around women that were out of order within their households. This looks like a woman carrying 10% of the family burdens while making 90% of the decisions in the household without consulting her husband. Additionally, this is a woman that does not have boundaries with her children, co-workers, or friends. Based on personal experiences, God is not happy with a woman that does not live in His divine order. Particularly, He is not pleased with a woman that does not honor her husband by allowing him to protect, guide, and to provide for his family. Although I have been out of order for a huge part of my life, I am now aware that, that is unacceptable and not in God's will. Therefore,

I have made a decision to live a life that consists of vulnerability, honesty, and authenticity.

Today, I have chosen a life with order and that resembles having a head of the household and a neck so that the head can move. Since I have identified my rightful role in our household, my husband and I are capable of making team-like decisions. I have witnessed first-hand how God blesses His children that trust and believe in His promises. Because we were willing to line up in our rightful order and step out on faith, I am living life more fulfilled. I am a woman of GOD first, a good WIFE (as my husband would say), a terrific mother (from my children), a working WOMAN (my co-workers would say) and I have a PASSION for Life. Therefore, I have made a decision to live a life that consists of vulnerability, honesty, and authenticity with my husband and children.

Sometimes God allows disorder in our lives so that he can place us in order to walk in purpose.

Reference

Hybels, B. (2009). Courageous leadership. Zondervan.

Testament, N. (1982). New King James Version. Nashville: Thomas Nelson Publishers.

Trimm, C. (2007). Commanding Your Morning. Charisma House.

Tiffiney Hodge
Author: Every Story Counts

Tiffiney Hodge is zealous about life and believes in surrounding herself with like-minded people. She is a member of the women's organization, Girls on the Grind, and a loving mother of three children. Her life's mission is to change lives one story at a time, through her writings and public speaking. You can reach Tiffiney at tiffiney_hodge@yahoo.com or call 614-717-3642.

STORY 11

EVERY STORY Counts

And once the storm is over, you don't remember how you made it through, how you managed to survive. You won't even be sure, whether the storm is really over. But one thing is certain. When you come out of the storm, you won't be the same person who walked in. That's what the storm's all about.

Haruki Murakami

Sitting on my bed, in a quiet house, I didn't want to think about any of the truths surfacing in my life at the moment; being unemployed, having a man who may be cheating on me, who can't help me financially, or how I was going to pay the monthly bills. The rent and car note were both due in a couple of weeks and once those were paid, a huge portion of my savings would be depleted. I knew if I did not find a job fast I would be getting an eviction notice and lose my car. All I wanted to do was go out and have a nice time with my cousin. I felt guilty about it but figured what it would hurt. After all, I had all week to soak in the miserable state I was in, as I had been for a few months now.

I was working as a customer service representative during the day and a bartender at night, five days a week; this had been going on for over four years now. When my bartending job began paying well enough for me to quit my day job, I quit. No notice, no nothing—just quit. Unfortunately, two months after that, the bar I was working for was undergoing new management. While away at a family reunion in Atlanta, I was called and let go from my job. It has been three months since I have had a job and I was getting by on a student loan check I received. So tonight, I was going to pretend my life was somewhat normal and leave my worries behind.

The heat was uncomfortable the entire day and I was relieved the cool night air was quickly approaching. I feared the last thing I wanted to do was waste time flat ironing my hair and putting on my makeup, only to head out the door and notice the transformation of a frizzed up pile of hair and my makeup appearing greasy from the humidity and sweat. I opened my bedroom window to allow a cool breeze to flow over my body. Now comfortable, I began shifting through hangers while trying to piece together an outfit to wear for the evening. I finally snatched the night's attire off the hanger and began laying each piece out on top of my bed.

My cousin Trina and I both lived for the weekends and truly enjoyed dressing up and getting loose on the dance floor to relieve the stress endured from the week's grind. However, this time around, something was different. I was not content. I shook my head at the thought of having nothing to look forward to after the night ended, or sadly, at all, for that matter.

But I made the decision to finish getting dressed anyway, sprayed some perfume on, and standing in the mirror, I was proof that one does not have to look the way they feel. I mirrored a beautiful young woman who looked as if I did not have a care in the world. Where there should have been dark circles and bags under my eyes from all the sleepless nights and crying, there were none. I reflected an all-black jumpsuit, with my black and gold jeweled stiletto heels; with accessories to match, my hair was flat ironed for a smooth finish, and my makeup was flawless. I said a silent prayer, thanking God that my hair behaved itself, and with my head held high I forced a smile on my face and headed out the door. Walking towards the door with one foot in front of the other, along my way out, I grabbed my bag, keys to the car, and out the door I went.

On the drive to my Cousin Trina's house, I decided to throw in a mixed CD to get me motivated, while I got my plans together. I wanted to stop by and scan the crowd where my boyfriend at the time was hired to deejay at that night. In all actuality, I wanted to make sure Natasha (the other woman Devin continued to cheat on me with) was nowhere in the vicinity. When I pulled up in front of my Cousin Trina's house, I called her cell phone and told her I was waiting on her outside. A few moments later, I could hear her flip flops popping against the street pavement, as she approached the car. With a cigarette in one hand, her bag and heels in the other, she managed to open the door and let herself in the car. Trina looked pretty as she always did and she was dressed casually cute. We always had a good time together and I thought tonight would be no different.

First thing she wanted to know was where we were going. I told her that I wanted to stop by this party Devin was hired to deejay for, and told her it was at the bingo hall here in town. She gave me a hard stare, the same stare a mother gives her child when she knows they have something up their sleeve. The only difference was: I'm not her child. "Trina, what you looking at me like that for," I laughed. "Tiffiney, I am pretty sure that the party you are talking about is the same party that Natasha and her family are throwing…" I intercepted the conversation and said, "Wait! What? Nah, he didn't say anything about Natasha's party." She continued," Well….don't go up there and just to keep tabs on him," she advised me.

Trina knew about the love triangle between me, Devin, and Natasha. How every time I would put him out he would run and crash over at her place. So, watching me parade after him just to make sure the other woman was nowhere lurking was not Trina's idea of a good time, and I don't blame her. It was not fun for me either. My intentions were to show up to the party right before it was over and hang out at a few other spots instead; but, that was definitely out of the question now. I did not like the idea of Natasha and Devin being at the same place at the time. Further, that he left out whose party it was. I did not trust them as far as I could throw them, which was not far at all.

I thought to myself, the nerve of this guy to actually invite me to Natasha's family's party. I was so heated, I could have steamed rice; in other words, I was highly upset at the thought of him not mentioning that vital information to me, but he perhaps figured if he told me I would forbid him from taking the gig. That is exactly what I would have done.

My foot felt like it was attached to an anchor; I could not speed fast enough to get to this party. Every street lamp post, porch light, traffic signals, and the other cars alongside me looked like an endless string of neon lights. I was convincing myself the only reason why Devin would invite me was to prove to Natasha that he does not want her anymore; also, he was not going to turn down any money—especially since he knew what a hard time I was going through financially. I must have been driving like a mad woman. There for a minute I zoned out. I went into auto pilot. I managed to get us to the party safely. I did not side swipe anyone's car or get a speeding ticket by the cops on our way there. I drove down Limestone Street, made a left on Pleasant Avenue, and then a right on Dayton Avenue and drove that up until I got to my final destination.

To make a long story short, we went inside the party, kicked it, showed out, and had a ball. Yes, I got a few stares from Natasha and her crew, but I expected that much. Overall, I had fun and was ready to go home and relax. Everybody started to make their exits but I decided to stick around and wait for Devin to get his equipment packed up, while Trina went outside to talk to her friend in the parking lot.

I stood around the stage waiting on Devin; he disappeared to the bathroom, and it was taking him awhile to come out. It dawned on me if Natasha was feeling any type of way, now would be the time to confront me; and, all it would take is for her to think I was trying to be argumentative; and a fight break out. I did not want that kind of problem. My sixth sense was telling me I should not be in there by myself. She had her family in the building while I had none. She must have read my mind because before I could make my exit, Natasha called my name. So, I turned around to face her. This was not the first time she wanted to talk and frankly, I was tired of talking, so I asked, "What do you want Natasha? You're going to tell me that you and Devin are still sleeping together?" She had this devilish smirk on her face and announced clear as day, "Yes we sure are." Her response was loud and clear as if she picked up a microphone and announced it on the air waves for the world to hear. My feelings were crushed. Was this the plan after all: Devin cowardly run off in the bathroom and leave her to break the news to me?

Before my second attempt to leave, I did have one last thing on my mind that I wanted to say; but, before I could get the words out, she shot toward me like she was about to smack me, so I did what I had to. The inevitable was starring me right in the face. I knew I was not getting out of there without a fight. My right fist was balled up and I reached out and touched her in the left side of her face and continued to punch her until her family members came to her rescue. The next thing I know I was being jumped by three other women. I could not feel any pain from them pounding away at the top of my head, kicking my legs, or punching my ribs. I had a handful of hair in one hand, while someone held part of mine in theirs. There were so many people involved and what may have lasted less than five minutes felt like a long twenty. I never seen a tornado up close before but I imagine it looked similar to any one standing by watching this fight go down. We banged it out and it felt like it was me against the world.

The full liquor bottle I was hit with nearly knocked me out. I laid there in the child pose position, as a warm stream of blood was pouring out from under my eye, creating a small pool of blood on the floor beneath me. There was something wrong, very wrong. My lower eye was split open like a loaded baked potato; my eye was closed completely shut. My hair was dismantled, clothes torn off. The beautiful accessories I added to complete my outfit was probably chopped up and flung somewhere on the dance floor. Before I decided to leave, I ran into the bathroom so I could pull myself together. Looking in the mirror, I no longer reflected the pretty young lady without a care in the world. The way I had been feeling lately had surfaced and took precedence in the mirror I looked in. In a rage, glass went flying from all angles as my fist connected with the mirror. Now my hand was bleeding and cut in three different spots, but I did not care. I was done.

A few phone calls were made to my immediate family after the doctor explained that I may need reconstructive surgery, but he could not determine for sure until the x-rays came in. As family and friends crowded my hospital bed, all I could do was sit there in disbelief over what happened to me. Not to mention, Devin never came to check on me. Confirmation, I was never anything to him in the first place.

The doctor delivered the news that I would not need reconstructive surgery and would only need stitches. However, my right side of my face was completely swollen and sat three inches off my facial bone. He explained to me that my right eye socket was fractured and there were tiny cracks around my eye socket which may result in some permanent nerve damage. He assured me that I would look the same as before with just a little scar left from the stitching; but it would take four to six weeks to heal. From the looks of it, I had no idea how my face would ever heal properly, but I had to take the doctor's word for it; I had no other alternative.

While trying to recover from a broken heart and injured eye, I prayed every day, all day, for two weeks straight…asking God to give me understanding and change over my life. The first thing he showed me during those two weeks was the true meaning of going through something. The second thing was he showed me myself. Lastly, he told me to trust in Him, not man.

Many of us say we have been through so many traumas, trials, and pains in our life, when in actuality, we haven't been through anything at all. We may have had bad things happen to us, but never actually gone through it. There is a difference. To go through something one has to start at the beginning all the way to the end.

It was put in my spirit that I had to start at childhood, and go from there, so each day I peeled away layers of pain and disappointments in my life. I discovered there were pain, anger, and fear still sitting there on the inside, which took residence in my self-esteem, my drive, my faith, and my self-respect. Our pains are much like food that goes undigested in our bodies. If ignored, it does not go anywhere. It remains there until it starts to rot and when left there too long, it begins to affect other bodily functions. A properly working body will take what is useful and nourishing from every meal, every experience, and dispose of any waste, which goes through our system. In other words, it comes out. An improperly working body will try to hold on to everything—both good and bad—without taking it through the proper process to allow it to go through the body.

There was still so much pain that I was holding on to in my life that I never tried to process and get it out of my system. Much like an archaeologist, I had to dig deep and with every trial, heartbreak, upset, and fumble that I found, I carefully analyzed and placed under a magnifying glass so I wouldn't miss anything. Every day, I sat home trying to connect the dots. My relationships with men were linked to my childhood molestations, and being a fatherless child, which in turn, gave me low self-esteem and a low sense of self-worth. As a result of having low self-worth, I attracted relationships with men and women who had low self-worth which resulted in domestic violence, back stabbing, terrible advice, lies, deceit, and so forth. Everything we do and how we see the world around us is in one way, shape, or form linked to something that happened to us in the past.

Once I understood how imperative it was for me to go through it all, I was more ready than ever to evict every negative past and present experience out of my life, once and for all. Not only did God give me an understanding of what it meant to go through something and how essential it is to start from the beginning all the way to the end, God showed me what I looked like to myself, and let me know I did not look like where I was going. I discovered that I was not my molestation, a runaway child, or pregnant teen, nor my past drug addiction, my lack of education, a sideline chick, my domestic violence, or my current income. Those were all things that took place in the course of my life, but they were not who I was.

By God showing me who I was, it was time for me to believe and have faith that where He was getting ready to take me was for my best interest. But I had to trust Him and not man. I practiced telling myself everyday how wonderfully and beautifully made I was and affirming good things to happen in my life. My focus shifted from negative to positive. Anytime I would go to a negative thought, I would counteract it with a positive thought. If I told myself, "I don't feel like getting out the bed, I'm tired," I would reverse it and say, "I am full of energy and can't wait to see what wonderful day God has in store for me." My life's perspective changed.

I was so consumed with my revelation from God that my situation with Devin and Natasha had taken the back burner. I wanted to change my life around, but I wanted a drastic change. When you want a drastic change in your life to happen you have to be drastic in your efforts. Yes, I wanted a change, a makeover. Not the kind of makeover when someone sees you and says, "Oh, how nice you look today." No, the kind of makeover I wanted was when somebody I knew would walk right past me without even speaking. My speech, my walk, and my appearance had to be unrecognizable. I did not just want to find a job; I wanted to find a job that I would like to do every day that would pay me more than I ever made. My old home had to look like a hut compared to the kind of home I wanted to live in now. That is the kind of drastic change I wanted to manifest in my life. People in my home town would have tried to admit me in an insane asylum if I told them what God was showing me of what my future looked liked.

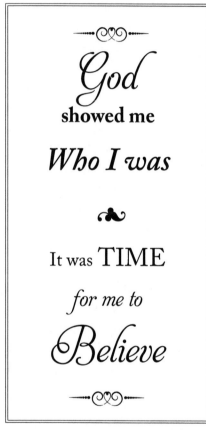

God
showed me

Who I was

❧

It was TIME

for me to

Believe

I remembered reading something on Facebook one day and it read, "In order to change, one has to be willing to be uncomfortable". That really hit home for me because I have always dealt with abandonment issues, never wanted to spend time alone with myself, and the older I got the less eager I was to find new friends. I thought being loyal to my friends was remaining who I always appeared to be because I feared that if I changed for the better, they would think I was trying to be better than them, when I was only trying to better myself. So, I was uncomfortable with that.

Sometimes we worry about other people's perceptions of who we are, more so, than we worry about what we think of ourselves. I said earlier that God revealed to me that I did not look like where I was going. Please keep in mind that after my relationship with Devin, many of the spectators and even some of my friends and family who knew I was being cheated on and used, and saw the fight that broke out after the party where I was injured. I may have looked like a mess; I was a single mother of two children, no job, just got beat up and injured in a fight over a worthless man, and made to look like the biggest fool known to man. Many of these same people knew my past, knew I had a history with cocaine use, had a reputation for getting in fights, cases of domestic violence, dated drug dealers, and hung out in the streets with some hardcore people—to say the least.

So, I did not look like to people in my hometown that I was going anywhere, anytime soon. I did not look like I was secure enough to leap out on faith and believe God had my front and my back. I did not look like in three weeks after I got beat up over Devin, I would be putting everything I owned on a U-Haul truck and moving me and my two kids to Columbus, Ohio, a major city an hour away from where I currently stayed. I did not look like someone who would do that with less than $20.00 to my name, no job, and no idea where I would end up. But who would have guessed that after two months of staying with my mother, who I had not lived with since I was 16, that God would bless me with a condo that included 3 bedrooms, 2 ½ bathrooms, a foyer, with an upstairs loft looking down into the living room, two huge picture windows, with 20 foot ceilings with a built-in fireplace, eat in kitchen, washer and dryer hook up, 2 car garage, move in ready, and the condo was less than six-years-old? I did not look like I was going to have a job that paid me on my one job more than what I was making with two jobs I had lost five months prior. All I know is when God's hands are in it, I will repeat it for the last time… you do not look like where you are going.

I learned the most from my relationship with Devin then I ever did with anything else that happened to me. Maybe because I was getting older or it was the straw that broke the camel's back. However, I knew that blaming everyone else for what transpired was not going to make anything better for the healing process. I knew I had to forgive all involved in order for me to have gotten to a place where I am today. In all actuality, I am glad that I lived through it because if I never made the decision to stick around after the party was over, who knows whether or not I would still be in that situation or still living in Springfield. I continue to learn everyday to pay attention when people show me who they are; I believe them the first time around. There are always signs that God will show you and alarms that will go off before you get in too deep, and I have learned to pay attention to those warnings today.

There is nothing about my story that one has not either dealt with personally or knows somebody who has. What went on during my relationship with Devin had all to do with how I valued myself, not just how he treated me. I was just as responsible for the incidents that took place in our relationship as he was, because someone can only do what you allow them to do. I heard the alarm go off and I chose to ignore it. My mother once told me,"When you play with fire, you will get burned." She was right.

I do not know what made you pick up this book and decide to read it. My guess is something may have happened or is happening to you in your life right now and you want some insight and knowledge. I hope that if you got anything out of what I shared with you on how important it is to process what you are dealing with from beginning to end, and trust after God shows you who you are, you believe Him as well.

Go ahead and get it out and actually go through whatever you need to. I advise people to write it out in a journal, or write a letter to the abuser and send it to China. Sometimes we have to go ahead and cry as hard as we can and fuss in the mirror until we get so tired. But whatever you do, do not ignore it. The pain can follow you in your everyday actions without even realizing it. It may seem strange telling someone who you do not know what is going on in your life; just talk about it to someone other than yourself. The wonderful thing about technology is it has allowed you to get free services without even having to leave the comfort of your home. It may be a good choice to Google 'free counseling services' in your area. Just promise yourself that you are going to take steps to get through it.

And just know that, everything happens for a reason and there's a time for everything (see Ecclesiastes 3:1-8). Keep balance in your life, stay positive, and affirm good things over your life. God knows your heart and he knows what it is going to take to get you out of your own way. So, even though it may be uncomfortable at the time, it is best for you.

The analogy, "you can plan a pretty picnic, but you can't predict the weather," no matter if you've never heard it before, or heard it a hundred times, is no less true. That for me is what makes life so mysterious. Life will either have you on the edge of your seat worrying about what is going to happen next or cheerfully anticipating your daily outcome. For most people, life is a mixture of emotions, obstacles, trials, and triumphs. The key thing to remember when going through rough times is that, "Life is not about waiting for the storm to pass; it's about learning to dance in the rain." -Author unknown.

Linda Michelle Trainer
Author: Rest Well

A possibility-thinker filled with a great passion for life, Linda Michelle Trainer is a flight attendant and founder and director of Elegant Doves International, Inc., a non-profit organization offering hope and healing from the repercussions of incest, abuse, and abortion. Her personal and professional vision is to see women and teen girls healed from emotional wounds, moving from their pain to their purpose. You may reach Linda Michelle Trainer by email at elegantlin@aol.com, through her website at: www.elegantdoves.org and by phone at 770-310-6434.

STORY 12

REST Well

Rest Well: The importance of taking time to renew your inner strength along your journey of purpose

Have you ever fallen up the stairs? You are on the move, heading towards accomplishing your task; focused, determined, and moving forward. All of a sudden, one slight misstep finds you tumbling face first into the stairwell, on your way up! After you pick yourself up, wipe the dust from your clothes, you simply readjust your stance, re-order your stride, and keep stepping forward to finish what you set out to accomplish. Now, however, you are more in tuned with where you place your foot at each step.

It is vital in our day to day journey to take time to stay in tuned with our steps or we run the risk of tripping over ourselves, head first, possibly causing injury and pain to ourselves and/or those around us. My "trip up the stairs" came in 2007, when I spent thirteen days in a mental health facility after being misdiagnosed as being bi-polar. What I actually had was adrenal fatigue, also known as adrenal exhaustion. The adrenals are two small glands that sit on top of your kidneys. Their job is to regulate your stress hormones, primarily adrenaline and cortisol. The adrenal glands give you increased focus and stamina to deal with sudden situations that require your full attention and effort. To cope with the stressors and strains on the body, your adrenal glands faithfully pump out extra energy for your body's use. Adrenal fatigue occurs when the adrenals reach the point where they are barely functioning. Some of the symptoms appear as extreme fatigue, depression, frequent illness, hormonal imbalance, and the inability to cope with stressful situations when they arise.

This "trip" of mine began several months before, when sitting in my gynecologist's (GYN) office hearing her review my results of a battery of tests she had performed. She told me my body was stressed. Doc, did I have to endure all of those tests and spend all of that money to hear you tell me something I already knew? She used the analogy of my body being like a car that was empty of gasoline. She said that I was forcing it to move, pressing relentlessly on the accelerator, and paying no attention to its warnings. During that time, my life was going full force, dealing with the pressing needs around me. There was the increased stress of my job and commute as a Flight Attendant, as well as the growing demands for services and training in my non-profit organization (healing issues of incest, abuse, and abortion). Additionally, there was the call to serve grand jury duty for three months, once a week. This was on top of supporting my husband as he experienced a major change in his career and the shock of hearing that my father was diagnosed with a terminal cancer.

The compound supplements and eating plan my GYN prescribed for me put a serious demand on my budget. I had to increase my hours at work to make the money to buy all I needed. That meant more travelling, being away from home longer, and adding additional travel time to check on my dad. The exercise my doctor recommended was put on the back burner because walking across the country (in flight) from New York to California at thirty-five thousand feet in the sky took most of my physical energy. As a result, my emotional energy was depleted even faster.

I developed an ear infection and proceeded to obtain a quick fix from an expert, who had no access to my medical records; nor did I have the strength or mind-set to fill him in on all of the aspects of what was going on in my life. I was only focused on having him stop the pain in my ears so I could get back to work. The antibiotics he prescribed were too strong for my weakened system. It was like putting jet fuel into a Mazda Miata. The visit to this expert took place less than two weeks after I visited my family doctor, who had prescribed a round of antibiotics he instructed me to take for 10 days. After six days and no noticeable relief, I took matters into my own hands and in my infinite wisdom, decided to enlist the help of the ear expert.

On my face I fell. Did I mention that this fall came after I put myself on a week-long fast so that I would receive revelation from the week-long, full-day spiritual conference at a local church? It had to be a sign from God that I was supposed to attend since it was taking place so close to where I lived, right? I didn't even have to travel out-of-state. Are you seeing the picture of the pieces of this puzzle taking shape here? How we can so easily take matters into our own hands, make quick assumptions, and take actions that we think are best without employing wisdom.

My fall came the Monday morning after that week-long conference and fast. Antibiotics, no sleep for about three days straight, and overflowing with new spiritual insights I didn't have time to process; I hit a wall. My heart felt as if it was going to explode through my chest and my mind was racing faster than the winning horse at the Kentucky Derby. The 911 operator talked me into going back inside my house to wait for the paramedic and not laying out in my driveway. I laid myself in the "recovery position" which I remembered from my first aid training, which really did help me to breathe better. The firemen and paramedics told me my blood pressure was very low, I was dangerously dehydrated, and I did the right thing in calling. I could hear a couple speaking with concern that I may have been suicidal because of the things lined up over my kitchen floor. I explained I put them there to help me to remember all that I wanted to share and write down when I felt better. My husband took a picture of it when he got home, after getting the call on his new job. He too expressed his concern when we spoke over the phone when he was able to finally reach me.

The first doctor I saw, a lady who looked to be in her tenth month of pregnancy, seemed to understand what was happening to me right away. The second doctor seemed convinced in his mind that something was wrong with me when I asked him to call my GYN, who could possibly help explain what was happening to me. I also mentioned my mentor, who I had worked with a few months earlier, enlisting her help in a counseling capacity to ensure I was properly processing my own past concerns when addressing the issues of the women who sought help from my ministry. In hindsight, I realize I had not discussed the overload of my schedule with her. The second doctor seemed to be offended when I mentioned anything with a spiritual connection and later told my husband that I was "spiritually brainwashed", which sent me into a "bi-polar episode". He suggested "72 hour observation" for my good, which he continued to extend out for a total of thirteen days…"for my good".

> *I was forced into a place to CRY OUT to God and afforded the Solitude to HEAR HIM SPEAK*

Romans 8:28 (AMP) says, We are assured and know that (God being a partner in their labor) all things work together and are (fitting into a plan) for good to and for those who love God and are called according to (His) design and purpose.

Although it took me awhile to realize it, I found my days in the hospital were a blessing in disguise. My life was transformed for the better, and it allowed the healing process of my adrenal system to begin. I was away from every form of routine care and concern of home and work. I ate three healthy meals each day, spent time out in the sun daily, and was in bed by nine o'clock every night. I had not followed that kind of routine in years. My body was able to rest and my mind became sharper than ever. My body had time to heal away from the demands and stress of life. I was forced into a place to cry out to God and afforded the solitude to really hear Him speak and to make sense of what He was saying.

Although not allowed by patients, one of the nurses allowed me to "privately" borrow a Bible that was kept at the nurse's station. The TV during the day was tuned into a channel which aired Joyce Meyer and Joel Osteen. In my desperation to try to make sense of why I was being confined in such a place (a shadowed valley) and not allowed to go home, my faith was confirmed anew to me. God was with me, although it took me time to sense Him. When the medication was flushed from my system and my mind was allowed to rest, I could hear the still quiet voice of God speak clearly to my soul. Some of the other women came up to me, out of the blue, asking me if I would pray for them. I was being filled afresh and even in that desert place, God was using me as an oasis to refresh others' souls.

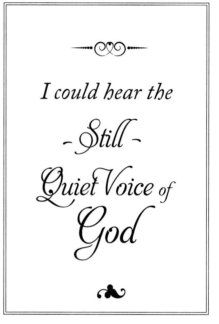

I could hear the -*Still*- *Quiet Voice* of *God*

I came to understand through this experience that I had violated not only some basic physical laws, but I had broken the simple spiritual "law" of not resting in God's presence. I had taken on the demands of my daily life and allowed fear to force me into working in my own strength to fix the broken things around me. The phrase "fear tolerated is faith contaminated" comes to mind. The time at the hospital and in the days which followed served in a sense as a spiritual detoxification. I was able to see how my stubbornness and pride had acted as poison to my spirit. I had been too busy to yield to the gentle nudging of God, often acting in my own strength as "Holy Ghost, Jr". God has His unique ways of getting our attention when He wants it, and He had mine.

It is true that "when your body is ready to rest, it will enter that rest with you or without you." During emergency situations of a decompression on an airplane, you are instructed to put on your oxygen mask before helping others. This experience taught me the meaning of the statement, "Your well-being is a prerequisite for the well-being of those around you." The same is true for you to remember as you move forward on your journey of purpose. Taking time to stop and rest enables you to hear your inner wisdom, the Voice of God. You will be better equipped to make quality decisions about your next course of action. You will be able to recognize this wisdom, even if it is being muffled by the chaos around you.

Tim Clinton, President of the American Association of Christian Counselors, shares a comment on Mark 6:31, which has become a lifeline for me. Under the caption of "Soul Note", in The Bible of Hope, Clinton writes, "Rest Stop: After an exhausting time of ministry, Jesus invited His disciples to 'come aside by yourself to a deserted place and rest a while.'" They took a break from their ministry in order to refresh themselves. A hectic schedule takes a physical, emotional, and spiritual toll on us. God knows that we need to come aside and rest a while so that we don't burn out. He will refresh us so that we can continue to serve Him. Rest and refreshment is not wasted time. Take time to rest, renew, and refresh your mind and your body. Use rest as a strategic power move to help you propel forward and healthier into your purpose.

WHEN I "THINK" I "THANK"

When I THINK about my GOD and all HE'S done for me

I just gotta THANK HIM for sending HIS Son for me

When I THINK about my GOD and all HIS ways

I just gotta bow down and THANK HIM and give HIM praise

When I THINK about my GOD, my Jehovah Jireh

I just gotta THANK HIM, because I haven't had a job since 2009

And HE'S been my sole provider

When I THINK about my GOD, the GOD that I serve

I just gotta THANK HIM for being a promise keeping GOD that backs up HIS WORD

When I THINK about my GOD it just makes me wanna shout

Because I was once was lost and turned out, but it was HIS love that brought me out

When I THINK about my GOD, the GOD that heals

I just gotta THANK HIM, because when the doctor said "Brain Tumor"

HE said "Daughter, that's not my will"

So when I THINK about my GOD, I just gotta THANK HIM

Because HE'S been too good to me for me not to open my mouth and praise HIM!

So when I THINK about MY GOD, I THANK HIM

By: Phaedra T. Anderson

About the Editor/Complier

Dr. Lily Jenkins is an author, professor, pastor, and entrepreneur of several businesses. She is the Co-Founder of the **Purpose Development Institute** and CEO of one of its subsidiaries, **Lady of Purpose Network.** She is the Founder & CEO of **UpgradeU Writing and Editing Services,** where she is a writing coach and a copy editor for authors and businesses nationwide.

Being the first female Certified Purpose Development Coach, Dr. Jenkins is on the leading-edge of helping individuals and organizations to discover a new dimension of purpose. Her experiences and insight to purpose allows her to speak directly to the voids that individuals face in the 21st Century. She is gifted in using purpose in both domestic and entrepreneurial matters.

Dr. Jenkins is also an accomplished author of 9 books and has been listed as a consecutive best-selling author on the Top 50 Black Christian Book Company Independent Publishers Bestsellers List for Non-Fiction and Amazon.com. One book awarded her a winner of the Pine-Sol Powerful Difference Contest. She was featured for her impact in the community with her anti-bullying campaign in *Ebony Magazine*, Dec./Jan. 2010 issue.

Dr. Jenkins is also a dynamic inspirational speaker who has been sought after by churches, writing circles, schools, and community organizations to motivate, encourage, and inspire today's youth & young adults. She has been featured as a writer on *The Review Magazine, Internet Cafe Devotions, Written Magazine, Booking Matters Magazine, Inspired Women Magazine, Live Magazine,* and *Kingdom Voices Magazine* is now a writer with *Preaching Woman.com* under the theme, "Ladies of Purpose", and *Success and Failure.net.* She has been interviewed on various radio shows, as well as *Atlanta Live Ch. 57 TV.*

Dr. Jenkins business savvy and leadership is a great addition to the Purpose Development Leadership team. Besides pioneering the Purpose Development message with her husband and a business woman who wears multiple hats, she enjoys being a wife and mother as they raise the bar of purpose for their marriage, family, ministry and business.

To order more copies of this or other books by Dr. Lily Jenkins, go to www.drlilyjenkins.com. Many of the books are also available on many online retailers and bookstores everywhere.

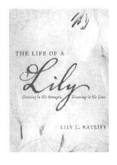

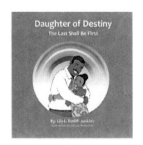

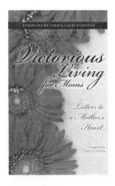
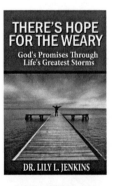
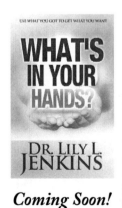

New Release! *Coming Soon!*

Ladies, join the Lady of Purpose Network!

www.ladyofpurpose.info

◆ Live Weekly and Monthly Calls

◆ Members Only Facebook Group

◆ Library of Purpose Development Training to include:

  ◆ Videos

  ◆ Audios for MP3 Download

  ◆ Downloadable Documents/Sermon Notes

  ◆ Discounts on Books, Trainings, and Events

Be able to join our affiliate program and earn a monthly recurring income. And so much more!

Be a part of a powerful network filled with women who knows what it means to be a...

Lady of Purpose!

CPSIA information can be obtained at www.ICGtesting.com
Printed in the USA
BVOW08s1714201113

336781BV00001B/2/P